STRATEGIC WORK

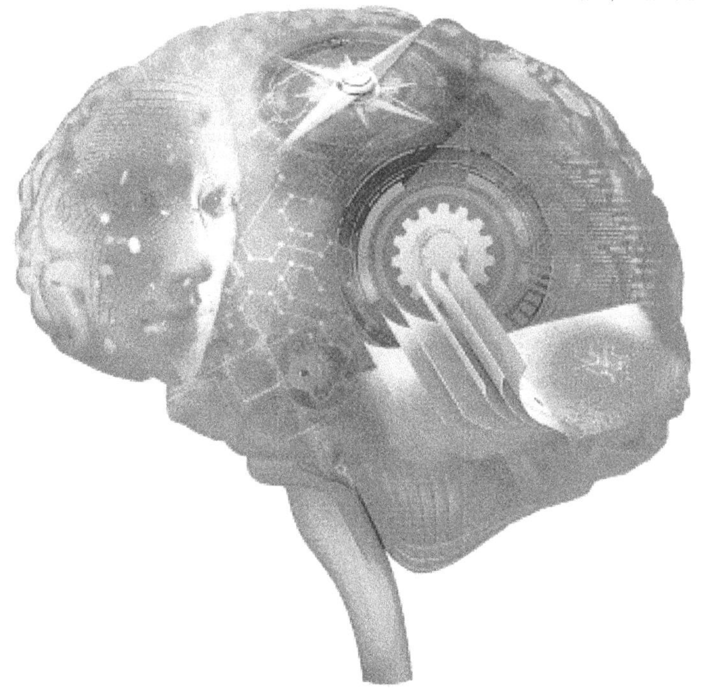

A COMPREHENSIVE GUIDE FOR SALES, BUSINESS DEVELOPMENT AND CORPORATE CULTURE

Marcus Deiss

ISBN: 978-3-9525174-8-2

Disclaimer

The author has used their best effort in preparing this manuscript for accelerated learning purposes. The book does not recommend specific tools because the organisation usually defines them. Instead, the subject matter and methods for determining the best course of action are provided in examples and are options. The accompanying materials provide accurate, authoritative information to inspire readers. The information herein contributes to further academic studies regarding the subject matter covered.

About the Author

Among a collection of academic credentials, Marcus also holds a diploma in Telecom Engineering (specialised in Telecom Transceiver Stations) and Economics, Commercial studies in Trade and Business Administration. Also, he is a certified precision mechanic and foreman in the field of metalwork.

Marcus lives in Switzerland with his wife and their two daughters. He is a former Swiss semi-professional football player who enjoys playing chess, reading and writing non-fiction books, on topics ranging from sales performance, business development, and corporate culture.

His passion has always been around helping people succeed, and his research interests are diverse, and cross multiple disciplines that broadly address narratives of employee experience and performance in B2B (business-to-business) workplaces, primarily in the IT, ICT (Information and Communication Technology) and Digital Signage sector.

Dedication and Acknowledgements

Much appreciation goes out to all who read this book. A special thanks to the organisations I worked with for all they have taught me. Moreover, I'm grateful to have met so many amazing people on these endeavours. I dedicate this book to students, sales colleagues, coaches, and consultants. Thanks to all who contributed to my learnings and for their aid that influenced this work.

Contents

PART I – Assessing Capabilities....5
Chapter 1 - B2B Leaders of Tomorrow....6
Development of Future Skills....7
Chapter 2 - Strategic Work Derives Legacies....11
Selling is Strategic Work....12
Chapter 3 - Building Your Sales Career....16
Will Technology Replace B2B Sales people?....18
From Sales to a CEO Legacy....21
Chapter 4 - Sales versus Business Developers....25
Chapter 5 - Business Models are Sales Strategies....31
Conceptual B2B Sales (or Solution Selling)....32
Scope (Deliverables/Inclusions/Exclusions)....35
Timeframe (Schedules)....36
Costs (Budget)....38
PART II - Due Diligence....39
Chapter 6 - Pre-Sales Phase of the Sales Cycle....40
Five Milestones of The Sales Cycle....41
Milestone # 1 – Generate and Qualify Leads....42
Milestone # 2 – Product Positioning....44
Milestone # 3 – Negotiations and Commitment....48
Chapter 7 - Post-Sales Phase of the Sales Cycle....49
Milestone # 4 – Deal Won (Contract Awarded)....50
Why Was a Deal Lost?....52
Milestone # 5 – Retain and Develop the Customer....54
Chapter 8 - Build Rapport Before Negotiating....55
Negotiations in the Sales Cycle....58
Exhibit Adaptable Consciousness in a Job Interview....61
Chapter 9 - Archetypes in Perspective....65

Understanding Social/Behavioural Styles....67
The Four Social/Behavioural Styles Approach....70
The CONTROL-Driven Style....71
The PEOPLE-Driven Style....71
The DATA-Driven Style....72
The CONFORM-Driven Style....73
Chapter 10 - Discover Power....75
Self-reflect for an Enhanced Future....76
Positive Mental Attitude Predictions....78
Chapter 11 - Source of Power in B2B Sales....81
Corporate Culture on the Top Shelf....82
Use Leverage for Sales Growth....85
Consider External Forces....87
PART III - *Develop an Action Plan*....89
Chapter 12 - Strategic Organisational Capabilities....90
Tools for the Sales Job....93
Chapter 13 - Key Performance Indicators....96
Your First Day on the New Sales Job....99
Chapter 14 - Sales Engagement Preparation Plan....104
The Preparation Plan....104
Customers' Decision-Making Process....108
Chapter 15 - Effective Communication is Active Listening....110
A Mindful Presenter....112
Chapter 16 - Cold Calling is Essential....118
Cold Calling Example....120
Dealing with Gatekeepers....121
The End....123
Glossary....124
Bibliography....128

Introduction

The rapid shift in customer behaviour is what drives change. Today, computers can make tactical judgments, sensor emotions, or even self-drive vehicles. They perform routine physical and intellectual tasks faster, better, and cheaper than humans. These cognitive abilities were once considered too difficult to automate. Yet, even after decades of robots and automation, we still lack evidence that humans someday might run out of work.

As we head towards the fourth industrial revolution in increased quality, speed, productivity, and flexibility, we also acknowledge that professions will appear while others will become outdated. Many traditional roles will be digitalised and managed by computers. However, this scenario still requires someone behind the computer, creating more job growth in new business sectors.

The technological enhancements that drive the fourth industrial revolution impact both developed and developing countries the same. All underemployed workers and low-end skill workers may not afford the goods artificial intelligence (AI) produces, and across all continents, workers with low-end skills are those with the highest risk of being replaced by robots and automation. Amidst all the benefits we envision in the fourth industrial revolution and its education system, we can imagine it will ultimately cause a massive displacement of people. Millions will be left without purposeful work, or well-earned skills will be rendered obsolete by organisations and governments that seek to cut costs for margin improvements. At this pivotal point, governments and organisations are on the cusp of educational and talent management renaissances in addressing these challenges.

Bringing our education system into the twenty-first-century requires taking the lead instead of lagging, actively seeking out new creative ways of doing things and staying in touch with our world outside of the education system. Yet, only a few educational systems are ready to experiment and explore a modern format to learning while others cling onto obsolete teaching methods despite many students still struggle when being taught the same stale way which is a standardised curriculum through individualised testing with a one-size-fits-all pace.

Our educational system and its individual testing model make little sense to today's digital native student who memorises facts for an exam even though they can have this information in the palm of their hand. This model is failing to teach students how to handle and respond to digital disruption and transformation. There are enormous unexploited potentials in schools, institutions, and organisations to how people can be creative to be successful. Besides that, teaching, learning and education have always been more than collecting degrees and diplomas. Just as leadership is more than getting others to achieve your own goals; their value lies in the quantifiable outcome one brings to humanity and the added value to the workplace.

While our personality, values, interests and ideas of success vary from person-to-person, our desire to live our lives without constraint is a universal one. To face the challenging environment automation, AI, robotics, and other cutting-edge technology brings, the twenty-first-century education system's purpose needs further evaluation to contribute to equality. Much of the disparities in living standards between developed and developing countries may be due to wide gaps in education that makes us more productive, increasing our income, and improving health and social integration. Governments have an obligation to continue to conduct extensive research and development surrounding futuristic skills where they might want to abolish obsolete degrees that will be less significant in the digital world and make efforts to raise enrolment rates and increase student learning options to significantly improve living standards in developed and developing countries.

What Can You Expect From This Book?

How can we achieve success in an economy where technology potentially takes jobs away and is programmed where all profits go to the robot owners? Which professions or tasks will be automated or become obsolete, and which trades are likely to endure? Will the tasks and jobs that become obsolete be creating new job opportunities, and which future skills will be in demand for these occupations? What qualifications will be the right fit for the fourth industrial revolution because a lifetimes debt is not worth paying if you end up struggling later to find a job after graduation? What profession can elevate your emotional intelligence and intuition to get a competitive edge in the digital era and fourth industrial revolution? These are just a few questions that will be covered in this book.

The manuscript proposes learning-options for youth and students thinking of a career in tech but don't know what profession to choose in the world of business-to-business (B2B). It explores why face-to-face occupations such as sales and business development professions are less likely to suffer the consequences of the fourth industrial revolution. It's also directed to millennial entrepreneurs and young salespeople who want to grasp a unique vantage point and a comprehensive understanding of business development and to prevent them from making mistakes or errors and the trouble of correction.

The approaches in this book have been confirmed in action so we can consider them valid. These principles and practices are based on two decades of research and validated by lessons-learned. They are taught to new members, presenting them as the appropriate way of thinking and feeling the challenges of strategic work in sales roles. The result is a step-by-step guide with a compendium of techniques and tools, including resources to harness the power of workplace-knowledge transfer for sales and business development.

When you finish studying this book, you will have a better understanding and a complete picture about the sales profession, allowing you to learn the sincerity about salespeople, and what separates a sales expert from a professional conversationalist.

Why Did I Write This Book?

My interest in questions such as the ones above emerged while working in different B2B sales roles and positioning cutting-edge technologies to vertical market segments for organisations that used a wide range of business models. I was not only amazed by the acceleration in cutting-edge technology over the past two decades, but I was also surprised at what I could achieve as a salesperson when using emotional intelligence and intuitive-predictiveness to resolve daily challenges with people and their problems.

My reading of popular books on sales and business development performance has supplemented my academic research and personal training as a salesperson. At the same time, I explored the world of strategies that shaped legacies and attended numerous training programmes. I enjoyed books like The Power of Your Subconscious Mind by Joseph Murphy, Good Strategy Bad Strategy by Richard Rumelt, Influence by Robert B. Cialdini and many more. These training programmes and books taught me the fundamentals, and for that, I am thankful for achieving my track-record. Since we all have wisdom and life experiences to share, writing a book also leaves behind a legacy.

How This Book is Organised

Though some chapters are interconnected, most are self-contained, so you can read the chapters that interest you first without feeling lost because you have not read the book from front to back.

The book is divided into three parts:

- In part I, we will explore why face-to-face occupations are less likely to suffer the consequences of the digital revolution. Readers will grasp the sales fundamentals and benefits of being in sales and business development.
- In part II, readers will learn the building blocks around sales strategies, human development and psychoanalytic theories. You will also learn countermeasures and social-cognitive characteristics to improve interactions with

people.

- In part III, you will learn the techniques and skills needed for sales, including the key performance indicators and the critical success factors for sales and business development.

For you to get more sense of approaches and techniques in the book, plan on reading chapters more than once. Have fun learning strategic work!

PART I – Assessing Capabilities

"Our vision of future success lurks behind a curtain, and until the curtain is raised, we can never have the complete image. We see in part and predict in part."

Chapter 1

B2B Leaders of Tomorrow

For many of us, our vision of the future is inspiring, filled with new technologies and new opportunities, but for some professions, the future these technologies foreshadow doesn't look as bright.

Industrial robots have evolved from dangerous industrial machines into smart, connected robots. They can analyse data more efficiently and make quick decisions to optimise production. Today, a cobot's arm can have seven-axes making it easy to replicate the human arm motion to move objects at a desired speed. This agility gives car manufacturers an extraordinary level of customisation to change everything from the car body components to the car seat type.

Cutting-edge technology will continue to absorb and automate repetitive tasks usually done by humans. It will redistribute labour across vertical market segments, and this is likely to cause additional economic disturbances. However, when adopting new technologies, we tend to narrow our view and lose sight of the human aspect. Though technology alters how work is done and who does it, most human to machine interface activities will still rely on people to program new and different things, such as programming a cobot's arm to complete a specific task or train a chatbot to provide better customer service. Therefore, even when cutting-edge technology is implemented, people play specific roles which won't change in the future.

Organisations and leaders who view technology as a tool to automate processes and displace its workforce may see short-term gains but will miss the full potential since technology's power should be to complement human proficiency, not replace humans. Naturally, the adoption of cutting-edge technology requires a strategic approach. The relevance of various disruptive technologies requires both human and technological capabilities because what comes naturally to humans (like humour) can be tricky for robots, but how machines analyse multiple gigabyte data remains nearly impossible for humans.

The same data-driven collaborative intelligence across multiple applications and domains that are crucial for the next generation of cutting-edge technologies to transition from feeble automation to robust automation is also adopted by B2B leaders of tomorrow (collaborative leaders) who embrace collaborative intelligence to improve their operational excellence, business models, and employees' engagement.

We may think that some leadership styles are more effective than others, but the truth is that each leadership style has its place. We will emphasise more on the collaborative leadership style due to them being common today. These are leaders that use a variety of engagement methods, and they brainstorm with their employees before implementing transformation. To fully benefit from collaborative intelligence, organisations should understand:

- How humans can amplify machines.
- How machines can intensify what humans do well.
- How to reshape business processes to support the collaborative intelligence partnership.
- How to identify the right technology that map business strategies to respond to the shift in customer demand.

The best ideas typically come from groups of people who pool their experience and expertise to further develop the organisation in which they work. These are concepts that reduce costs and improve internal collaboration making the organisation more agile to improve productivity, and to reveal new market opportunities in reaching different customer segments.

Development of Future Skills

Though technology has created more jobs than it has wiped out, about half of the activities (not jobs) carried out by workers could be automated. Some analysts suggest up to 50% of all professions could be automated to the extent that these jobs would finally disappear. While others estimate anywhere from 45%-60% of all European workers could see themselves displaced due to computerisation by 2030.

- In December 2017, a McKinsey & Company study found that about 30% of tasks in 60% of occupations could be computerised.
- In February 2018, a global PWC survey found that 37% of workers were worried about the possibility of losing their jobs due to automation.
- A recent OECD estimates suggest that 14% of all jobs across the 32 OECD countries analysed have a high risk of automation. A further 32% of jobs may experience significant changes in how they are carried out.

It is then no surprise that there are several movies, books and many doomsday predictions on how technology will destroy our world. We've all seen sci-fi movies like The Matrix where robots take over, and humans fight over the remaining ways of life. Technology will continue to evolve and disrupt the workplace and the workforce. Yet, as history unfolded itself, every time new technology or trends arose, there were questions raised around its usage for good or bad. As a result, society as a whole adapts, and this is what we continuously go through to evolve as humans.

It's becoming clear that only good politics and governance will keep this dangerous doomsday scenario from becoming a reality. Politicians cannot disregard scientists and analysts who study this phenomenon. They should open their ears to the call to look for alternatives. We can find a similar phenomenon today in the animal kingdom, in which animals are worth more dead than alive. As long as our economy works in that way and organisations go unregulated, they are going to continue to annihilate animals. Therefore, if our society cannot agree on what is truly right or that there is no such thing as truth, then we can't navigate out of any problem.

As our workplace continues to move from manual labour to online roles requiring more critical thinking and planning, the worker of the future will increasingly have ICT knowledge in areas like programming, creativity, and strategy. Though technology may reduce the pool of available jobs, there are many potential upsides to this transformation. We are in the age of start-ups and technology-driven business with remote workers where innovation allow almost any job to be divided into specific tasks for which workers are paid at a rate determined by the work demand at a given time. Amazon's crowdsourcing service platform called Mturk is an excellent example. Organisations and researchers pay workers ("turkers") to complete minor tasks. Computers cannot do these tasks called Human Intelligence Tasks (or HIT). Tasks such as helping train an algorithm, identifying objects in a picture, transcribing an audio recording, or identify a tweet tone etc. However, the worst-case scenario would be that the wealthy few continue to dominate over the unemployed masses. As always, only public policies and good governance will dictate the trajectories of economic growth and wealth distribution.

As governments and businesses streamline their strategies and pivot during the COVID-19 pandemic, our workforce and work environment will continue to transform. The COVID-19 pandemic showed how dependent we are on digitalisation and on doing all processes online. COVID-19 did more for digitalisation than any government or leader of a large organisation could have ever done. There is no doubt that COVID-19 changed our way of life, and we must now accept living with the pandemic as we survive and strive in the new normal. The pandemic was a real-time test environment, and we acknowledged that on certain aspects, we were ready while on others, we still had work to do. We were more exposed to cyber-attacks, some even lost trust in the media and their government due to fake news. We saw opportunities with COVID-19 in products that suddenly became more in demand such as cleaners or disinfectant products. COVID-19 brought tremendous change to the way we work, the way businesses communicate, collaborate and engage.

Whether new technologies or trends, people and time management remain the most critical operation to balance, is the idea then outdated for millennials to be in the office at 8:30 sharp and get paid by the numbers of hours they spend at their desk? Some may envision the 60/40, 70/30 or 80/20 sales commission rule as a workable option for other departments of an organisation because when an employer sets a salary, they are thinking value not necessarily time. That said, millennials ought to be more purposeful about their profession choice since they are arguably the most blessed generations that can be transformative, not necessarily all in a positive way. They have all the technological access, on-demand self-learning capabilities and extreme social networking. They are the largest generation in the workplace, and they have joined Gen-Z to be characterised as the most stressed-out working generation today.

Burnout, purpose and passion may not seem connected, but there is a connection. Though efforts have revolved around how to promote employee engagement, in at least nine European countries, burnout is recognised as an occupational disease. Organisations, research institutes and regulators should re-evaluate this approach, finding a way to avoid burning out employees in the process. The higher the workload demands, the more support and opportunities for recovery the employee needs. An organisation's wellness programs with fitness, yoga, or free stuff are not the primary way to respond to stress since a much more significant source of tension remains the workload itself and how its managed. Burnouts have no preference, and it can happen to anyone who is passionate about their work. It can happen to anyone who works with an element of risk, or even an individual that operates in a socially isolated environment. We regularly hear about burnout in one profession or another, yet burnouts will continue to exist as our society values 24/7 availability and short-term gains. Also, remote work contributes to the stress and the burnout epidemic.

In addition to burnouts, workers of the future may also face challenging times to identify themselves with an organisation; however, upwards career trajectories and job opportunities will finally define a dream job, but their biggest struggle revolves around finding their passion. Finding a passion friendly work environment and a chance to earn more can be challenging, but thankfully, there are ways to find your passion even in a job that's less than perfect:

- Speak to your boss about other opportunities.
- Identify a mentor you can learn from and ask questions.
- Control your trajectory and get yourself a new degree or certification.
- Volunteer or seek interactions that make you feel good.

Though following your passion can help open doors to your dream job, this static mindset of putting all your efforts into one area will more likely end up in you dropping it all or giving up when obstacles arise. Many stories exist of people who didn't follow their passion. Steve Jobs was passionate about Zen Buddhism before entering technology. Heather Russell, the founder of Biscuit who stated, "Was I passionate about real estate when I started? Absolutely not. However, we found an opening in the market and decided to build a solution for it. And then I had to develop a passion for all the things associated with that market."

While obsessive passion is adaptive, following your passion can lead you to stray. It doesn't usually help you find your dream job since one's passion (or interests) remains static, and they don't develop as we and the world around us evolves. Besides, the primary path to passion is doing things that expand your comfort zone without leaving you in constant fear.

We all have different perspectives of passion and success, yet still, we have the same envy for a stable job at a thriving organisation with an inclusive leadership style that encourages us to work at our very best. A dream job can be one that makes the most out of your qualifications and abilities in a fast-paced and friendly work environment that empowers you to make decisions, having authority over budgets, practices or strategy. It should be challenging where you learn new topics, and of course, job opportunity enhancements to develop your career further.

Chapter 2

Strategic Work Derives Legacies

Salespeople and business developers are in the best position, with an ideal ability, to create legacies for their employer and themselves. Legacy building in the business context comes from working to ensure the long-term sustainability of the organisation and leaving it more durable, more efficient, and more valuable than it was before. In more dramatic scenarios, salespeople might lead the creation of an entirely new product or services for the organisation that could potentially bring in millions in revenue.

We can especially define legacy as the knowledge, skills, beliefs, or behaviours people take away as a result of having worked with you. This legacy is not only a benefit to the organisation; it's also part of one's professional career brand.

Legacy represents the most challenging and most rewarding endeavours of your career. No matter who you are, in other people's stories, you have likely been both a hero and a villain. John F. Kennedy, for instance, left behind a legacy of positive actions while Hitler left behind a legacy of terror and destruction. Both are equally essential for lessons learned. A legacy grows with each endeavour, with each bold, untested concept that you are brave enough to implement, and with each time you inspire others.

To create a lasting legacy and a sustainable business strategy, leaders inspire their employees with a sense of meaning and purpose. According to experts who have studied leadership for decades, the most significant parts of a leader's job is to have a distinctive and unique prediction that can exalt a vision of the future. For instance: when Tim Cook continued to uphold Steve Jobs legacy at Apple, or when the Amazon founder (Jeff Bezos) acquired the Washington Post, Jeff will not only carry on its legacy but build upon an effort to transform the newspaper to the modern era, or when the founder of Virgin Group (Richard Branson) had it right when he said he wants his legacy defined as someone "To have created one of the most respected companies in the world. Not necessarily the biggest".

When we think about it, legacy is the establishment of customs passed on to future generations. This model in a family business is directly passed on to family members to take over and further grow the business successfully. The CEO is then responsible for upholding the legacy customs that came before them, so long as those customs benefit the organisation. Simultaneously, they hold themselves accountable to those customs to strengthen the organisations brand.

When the term CEO was introduced in the 1990s, leaders operated as autocrats whose visions, strategies, and customs were handed down. As the CEO role evolved to become more decentralised through building executive teams, monitoring performance, and to oversee the allocation of resources, leaders' legacy accomplishments differed from their autocratic predecessors. Today, even the brightest CEOs struggle to create legacies amid the disruption and chaos of the globalised market, and above all, the immediate task of creating shareholder value. The intense pressure from stakeholders to meet immediate financial goals takes away time leaders would need to evaluate strategies for the future state of their organisation and their power to build long-term value. Subsequently, many CEOs fall into obscurity the moment they depart their organisation. Given the accelerating pace of change, would now be time to let go of the ideal of the CEO as a visionary?

Selling is Strategic Work

It's brilliant, perhaps even visionary of how salespeople can create business development strategies that derive legacies. In reality, a business development strategy considers the engagement between all internal departments (e.g. sales, marketing, customer service, finance, operations etc.) and external factors (e.g. customer relation, competition, market opportunities, trends etc.) that enable the organisations to grow and maintain success. It's a document that describes the actions an organisation takes to accomplish their goals. The business development strategy is primarily about deciding what is truly important and focusing resources and actions on those specific objectives. A great deal of the work in business development is trying to figure out what is going wrong, then making it right – and not just deciding what to do, but identifying the root cause to avoid it from happening again.

Business development strategies are competitive assets designed for the long-term; they are usually created and executed by salespeople, designed to be agile and are determined over time based on various predictions, success and fail indicators. In essence, a business development strategy presents short, mid-and long-term milestones to help sales teams identify the gap between current performance and the value management wants to achieve. The design of a business development strategy is an activity-based on lessons learned, theory and predictions, and it produces real results on the front lines when put successfully into practice. The reason design is discussed here is to emphasise the matter of adjustments. In design problems, where various elements are planned, adjusted, and coordinated, there can be large wins to getting the combinations right and sharp costs when getting them wrong. In other words, designs are more constructed than chosen due to building upon the lessons learned, but only a few are willing to exert the effort to undergo this design process.

To begin designing a business development strategy, let's look at the basics of strategy from a different perspective. Imagine a situation where you are ill, and you visit your doctor. The doctor's goal is to restore your health through the practice of medicine. The challenge your doctor faces appears as a set of symptoms. Based on the symptoms perceived by the doctor and information from the patient's history, the doctor makes a diagnosis, naming the cause and effect of a disease. The doctor then decides on a course of action, which could be prescribing medication or a healing therapy, to achieve the goal of making you healthy again. The same approach applies to the design of a business development strategy or for that fact, for any strategic work. In the context of designing a business development strategy, you should understand and consider the following:

1. The three elements of vision (short-term, mid-term, and long-term).
2. The three elements of strategy: (i) Assess (Evidence), (ii) Predict (Logic), (iii) Plan (Conclusion).
   - Assess (What EVIDENCE exists?): The salesperson conducts an assessment of the current situation based on organisation intern lessons learned (e.g. organisational targets, customer order history, etc.) and external factors (e.g. competition, trends, etc.).
   - Predict (Predictions in the LOGICAL sense): The customer order history makes it easier for the salesperson to make predictive forecasts for the coming year. Also, with the order history and an understanding of the customer relationship, they get the big picture of their organisation's strengths, weaknesses and they might have identified obstacles they need to overcome to achieve their goal.
   - Plan (CONCLUSIONS will inform the Action plan): The salesperson then creates and executes an action plan to overcome obstacles discovered to achieve their predicted-vision.
3. The understanding of the target audience (interests, archetypes, etc.) and what they know (e.g. products and services) and think (e.g. good or bad assumptions) about your organisation.
4. The two theories on how your organisation processes work:
   - The leader's theory (centralised): The leader's theory begins with an assessment of the opportunities and threats coming from the external environment and its available resources, including the amount of change happening. They follow up with a SWOT analysis. In this process, leaders first assess their environment and other indicators that are both positive and negative. They identify opportunities to minimise the organisational pain of its weaknesses or threats.
   - The employee's theory (decentralised): The employee's approach

comes as a series of lessons learned, predictions, and challenges amongst competing values, beliefs and KPIs within the workplace.

Designing and implementing a business development strategy should be at the top of your list of priorities as a sales leader if you want to get results and motivate your sales team.

Selling is strategic work, and it has been around since ancient times. Though dynamics then differed from sales today; the wheel, the chair, the clock or the Carnival in Rio de Janeiro that first occurred in 1723 are all old achievements humans consumed and were the result of successful strategic work. Strategic work can be an activity to design your business strategy, whereas tactical work is the activity you do to implement the design created by strategic work. Strategic work can be done to create a product or services demand and is usually used to achieve a specific goal, results or project outcome. For example, we learned of the various ideologies and strategic work for decades that helped achieve economic growth in various countries and continents:

- The Chinese New Year in 2019 contributed to 1 trillion-yuan (€ 128 billion) in revenue during the holiday period.
- The exhibition and conference centres sector in Australia was estimated to have generated revenue of $17.2 billion (€ 10.5 billion).
- Since 2016, the Brazil carnival exceeds 7 billion Brazilian reals (€ 1.24 billion) and creates 25 thousand temporary jobs every year.
- The Munich's Oktoberfest in 2019 was worth € 1.23 billion in total commercial revenue.
- In 2018, the NFL's championship game made $482 million (€ 407 million).
- The 2017 Cape Town (South African) carnival made an economic impact of R14.14 million (€ 2.25 million).

We acknowledge that each continent and country strives for dominance by competing ideologies and has its culture, characteristics and its calling to contribute to the human condition in a way that is unique to their life experiences and views.

Many countries should continue to unlocked the potentials combining sports, culture, or entertainment activities that derive legacies. We can imagine post-COVID-19 that both developed and developing countries will implement policies and systems that support similar ideologies and development for economic growth. In particular, African countries can benefit the most when combining football and cultural synergies to boost their cultural tourism sector through more events. Fact is football and cultural activities in Africa go hand in hand since the individual African can belong to unique or numerous tribes. Traditions in football and culture are tremendous, and opportunities exist to achieve more significant social and economic impact, yet many opportunities in developing countries remain untapped.

However, the road to sports and cultural synergies is paved with challenges, and it must be clear that success in competing ideologies is a destination that does not yet exist in Africa. But what is unacceptable is the unwillingness to learn lessons from poor governance and be stubborn in the face of all rational economic practices. Poor governance means governmental development initiatives have no adequate systems in place to develop that specific area. The warning signs of poor governance are widely known in Africa; tribalism, corruption, excessive borrowing, repression, constitutional violence and decline in domestic income are symptoms of failing governance.

Chapter 3

Building Your Sales Career

Why should you consider a career in sales? Because it offers personal satisfaction, financial rewards and ever noticed how our lives evolve into sequences of negotiations and results, where the universal sales skill became the core of all strategic work with people and their problems.

Millennials thinking of a career in tech but don't know what profession to choose should ask themselves the question if they want to pursue a degree yet will end up struggling later to find a job after they graduate? Other important questions arise, such as which occupations or tasks are likely to disappear in the future and which ones are likely to endure? Will the tasks and jobs that become obsolete be creating new job opportunities, and which future skills will be needed for these occupations? How will this degree help you achieve your career goal after graduation? Is this a degree that will be in demand for top employers? Think about what your career goals are by entering your degree of study. Though figuring out your career goals and how to finance your education can be challenging, there is help. Most students require financial aid to pay for college expenses. Several types of financial aid exist, and each is different in how it awards financial assistance. However, part-time employment in sales, for instance, can be tailored around the students' study schedules to help students cover these expenses.

While the educational system can be one of your best life experiences, choosing the right degree is crucial. There was once a time when any degree would set you apart from other candidates. Today, those learned skills (or degree) can soon become outdated with the rapid speed of technological progress we see. Though the value of a degree varies from country to country and major to major, the insights gathered here is more than just a degree. For instance, by showing up on time for classes, adapting to demands of different professors, doing the essential work of learning, coping with the stress that comes with exams, socialising with others, sharing ideas and debating on opinions are all valuable life experiences too. The educational system should be a time that enables you to explore yourself, to take risks, to learn and grow.

Sales and business development roles are stable professions, and some find sales jobs provide significant personal and professional gratification while others feel being in sales is considered a mediocre occupation as there is also a bias against them where they feel discomfort calling themselves a salesperson. Nonetheless, sales roles can be one of the top-paid jobs at an organisation, and they can offer excellent work-life balance and opportunities for further career progression. Sales can be a very fulfilling profession when you have the right leader, a top organisation and the right tools for the job. Professions such as Accountants, Auditors, Cashiers, Financial Analysts, Lawyers, Rental clerks, Drivers, and Telemarketers are at more risk in the fourth industrial revolution. That said, you don't have to pursue a career in sales as long as you can equip yourself with future-proof skills and a trade that will be in demand in the digital world because what is a lifetime's debt worth repaying if it doesn't guarantee you a job after graduation.

The B2B sales labour market demand continues to transform since the advent of the commercial internet over 20 years ago. Its influencing everything from the sales team structure to the strategies and tactics to engage with customers. Some labour domains are experiencing rapid job expansion, while others experience a declining outlook. These technological dynamics and skill demands are set to become the primary drivers of new job opportunity growth. Even though they pose challenges to best practice sales methods and existing business models.

Maybe some psychological aspect of being in sales lies behind the hundreds of books written from the early 20th century. All professions are not perfect, and all jobs are not easy, yet there are many advantages of being in sales. Sales will always be a beneficial skillset, especially as we see the need for control over our destiny in becoming entrepreneurs which is a dream job in itself. There are many other advantages to being in sales - some of which include:

- Sales job opportunities are unlimited. You can potentially work for any organisation anywhere around the world and have multiple workplaces.
- Sales jobs offer unlimited options for growth in responsibility and compensation. There is usually no capped compensation in many organisations. That said, a salesperson can sell as much as they want and get compensated (and promoted) accordingly.
- Salespeople get the latest tools and technology to do their job, and they usually get a company car they can also use for private purposes.
- Though salespeople work in regular office hours, they have flexible schedules to achieve their KPI's, and they have the liberty to choose where they work.
- Every day is a new adventure as they travel nationally and internationally. They visit new towns and cities where their flights and hotels are paid for. They get to meet people from all walks of life and from different cultures.

Will Technology Replace B2B Salespeople?

Technology can tap into virtually every aspect of a business's operations, and it's an essential element for turning business continuity into a competitive advantage. For that reason, many multinational retailer organisations that operate a chain of hypermarkets, discount department stores, and grocery stores, already have self-checkout terminals with plans to install more. Despite efforts by many retailers to automate more of their operations to reduce labour costs, they fall further behind to the online retailers whose marginal labour costs are close to zero. This raises the question of how long retailers will compete against online retailers with their substantial expenses.

The innovation and technology moving the automation market to near zero marginal labour costs will do the same to the human labour market. Innovation and technology are replacing human labour across the agricultural sector, production industries, learning sector, services-and-entertainment sector, and many more industries. The fact is that machines have been replacing human labour for centuries to automate physical skills. We saw this with the introduction of the printing press or the development of internal combustion engines. Since then, machines have continued to push out humans from manual activities.

While warehousing, shipping, and back-office workers are candidates for automation, the emotional intelligence and intuition to build customer relations are what can spare salespeople from being replaced by technology. We should question this trajectory of economic value in the digital age, and we ought to be concerned about our future professions as this environment changes. In the next few years, more tasks and jobs will go to technological enhancements that were once considered a regular route of professional employment; consequently, people could be forced to change their profession to get work. For example, both developing and developed countries have workless factories run by computers. We see the automotive and steel industries are replacing factory workers with automation, and it's becoming the norm. Though technology has lowered the workforce in the automotive and steel industry, we still see the automotive production continue to rise while the number of workers continues to decline.

China, India and Mexico learned quickly that the cheapest workers are not as economical, efficient, and productive as the automation that replaces them. Many large Chinese manufacturers are replacing low-cost workers with even less expensive robots. For instance, Foxconn is one of the largest manufacturers that produce smartphones, TVs, game consoles, and other IT/ICT hardware equipment that had announced plans to install one million robots over a 3-5 year period to minimise a large proportion of its workforce.

It's becoming ever harder to identify what jobs are or are not at risk. Development in innovation and technology means new roles get formed while others disappear. Processes which previously took a long time to complete are done faster and more efficient. Websites and automatic ordering systems are replacing millions of activities. We also see the loss of basic jobs in retail and fast-food sector through order-taking machines that have replaced them. Technology has displaced cashiers and retail salespeople whose tasks were also information-gathering from prospects and customers.

Today, the salesperson's role has transitioned into facilitators of the ordering systems rather than leaders of the sales cycle. The future doesn't lie in improving the performance of average salespeople and their current strategies. Instead, it involves altogether changing how salespeople interact with prospects and customers. To accomplish this transformation, organisations are taking their training and talent management to the next level.

That said, is the sales job a dying profession you should avoid? No, sales jobs are not disappearing anytime soon. However, traditional salespeople in the digital environment may have a disadvantage versus a selective group of B2B salespeople that are flourishing in conceptual B2B (or solution selling) sales environments. They don't only sell more effectively, but their sales approach is less selling than advising. These conceptual B2B sales professionals have abandoned many traditional sales jobs, and the wisdom taught in sales training programmes since this doesn't work well within conceptual B2B sales methods (see Chapter 5 - Business Models are Sales Strategies). The B2B sales job itself will not disappear so long as organisations offer products or services people want to buy. While technology may replace many sales activities, there is still a desire for human interaction when making a purchase. Sales will remain essential to business development because if you are not selling you will not be doing business for long. You could use technology to grow your sales pipeline, but ultimately you are not going to close more deals, nor will you be able to shorten your sales cycle, without a person speaking with the potential customers to finalise the sale.

While programmers are finding ways to make robots seem more human, salespeople should welcome these technologies as tools to help them do a better job, not replace them. Salespeople should embrace all types of technological transformation that support their sales activities, but they should avoid being driven into technology-led relationships. Digital methods are useful in many circumstances, yet they should be complementary to rather than replace conventional human interaction. The few technologies that come close still lack the human qualities necessary to build a real relationship. Robots cannot build rapport in a face-to-face meeting, nor can they understand the small distinctions that make or break a deal. As a result, salespeople should continue collaborating with customers in all ways humanly possible, such as:

- Asking questions: Customers don't expect salespeople to know everything about their business sector, which means salespeople should not fear to ask clarification questions, make mistakes, or take risks.
- Using data to form bonds with customers: In a digital world, data, research, and statistics contribute to the information needed to help cultivate the customers and even win them for life.
- Learn to listen: To compete in the twenty-first century, salespeople should not cut customers off, let alone start formulating responses while the customer is still speaking. Also, listen to learn and keep an open attitude free of prejudice,

discrimination, or emotions that can disrupt your listening experience.

- Sharing personal accounts and experiences: Building a relationship is a two-way street. So that they can be a connection, reveal something unique about yourself.
- Relationships within an organisation and with customers are about trust. Salespeople make sure that when they promise something, they and their organisation can deliver it.
- Salespeople have pearls of wisdom based on experience that computers can never match. This makes troubleshooting to find solutions easier, and this will remain more pleasant for the customer.

Today we see artificial intelligence-powered chatbots with some sales capabilities and other related technology that replace menial labour work. But, this scenario will not replace B2B salespeople that sell complex B2B end-to-end solutions due to:

- The complexity of end-to-end B2B solutions. It's challenging to understand all the different components that make up an end-to-end B2B conceptual solution. Also, the sales cycle duration, from the initial customer contact, to gain insight into the customer's demands, to provide a proof of concept with a test environment, to the final negotiation and closing of the deal is so complicated that specific events are unpredictable, engendering many surprises.
- Successful selling requires emotional intelligence, intuition, patience and perseverance. Face-tracking technology can help robots somewhat achieve a similar effect on emotional intelligence. But, it will still be challenging to replace where the humans and robots see eye to eye because we use eye contact to initiate and control communication. Displaying patience, perseverance and engaging in conversation involves looking in someone's eyes as they speak indicates that they have our full attention and keeps both parties engaged.
- The creativity and feeling to close the deal. Human communication and relations are extremely complicated occurrences, which makes the selling act itself very difficult. Many salespeople have been in situations where the prospect seemed entirely ready to award the contract but then backed out at the last minute. Something went wrong, but the salesperson was probably able to calibrate their approach to fix the situation and finally close the deal. Robots cannot intuitively and actively improvise very well to pivot when surprises occur.
- Garbage in is garbage out. Your robot or software tool is only as good as the data you gather and can only act based on the information you feed it. When adequate data is missing the robot cannot decide to collect the missing data to improve its skills. Instead, it waits for new programming languages from its master. Humans have an infinite ability to self-correct using their good judgement to make decisions.

- Networking and socialising: Regardless of how cute humans make robots, imagine hanging out with friends and a creepy robot. This might not be much fun when invited over for cocktails. Robots lack the social skills to make a positive first impression. It's hard for them to have a productive conversation that ends up with an exchange of contact information for future interactions. Above all, just imagine robots conducting a business lunch. Can you imagine an intelligent conversation with a customer over a plate of pasta without making the buyer feel unnatural? Though we already have robots that help us at home, and one can imagine talking to a robot won't be uncommon in the near future as people become older and lonelier. Especially as we age, we require help and can appreciate having something around us.
- Global trends: While COVID-19 and other economic trends lead to customer meetings and negotiations taking place online with videos conferences, this remains a human factor similar to a face-to-face meeting.

B2B salespeople shouldn't worry about robots taking their job. Instead, smoothen your B2B sales skills with effective training programmes and your future in sales and business development will be a captivating and gratifying experience.

From Sales to a CEO Legacy

Many stories exist about people who worked as sales reps early in their career before stepping into the CEO's office. Some of the most known examples are:

- Warren Buffett's began his sales career as a paperboy. Warren was the world's richest person in 2008, and one of the top 5 wealthiest people in the world.
- Howard Schultz started his sales career at Xerox selling word processors. He bought Starbucks in 1987 and grew Starbucks' revenue to $19.16 billion in 2015.
- Mark Cuban sales career began by selling software. He established MicroSolutions that grew to $30 million and sold it to CompuServe.

Several studies have uncovered roles people held before leaping to a CEO position. For instance, data pulled in 2017 based on information recorded by over 12,000 LinkedIn members who were CEO's at organisations with more than 50 workers and located in the following countries: Argentina, Austria, Belgium, Chile, Denmark, Finland, France, Germany, Italy, Japan, Mexico, Netherlands, Norway, Singapore, South Korea, Spain, Sweden, Switzerland, UK, and the USA. To note; this analysis did not represent all CEOs globally but was rather used to validate a way of learning together. The data showed that business development, by far, was the most common first job function of a CEO. It was twice as high as the second-most frequent function in sales followed by the third being engineering.

While we may know stories of legendary CEOs who started their career in sales, it's not uncommon for many CEOs to have finance, engineering or other backgrounds. Choosing a CEO with a sales background poses its unique challenges because salespeople typically take a fast-paced, agile leadership approach. They create valuable win-win partnerships, penetrating new markets, and increasing the bottom line by balancing short-term profitability objectives to achieve long-term sustainable goals. That is an excellent approach to leadership in many organisations as it helps grow business rapidly. Depending on the organisations' maturity, in some cases, choosing a CEO with a sales background might not work well since that leadership style can be disruptive in a more traditional, established organisation where more emphasis is on stability than on growth.

Organisations might be missing an essential pool of talent for the CEO role, considering that succeeding as a CEO relies on the ability to connect with others. This makes it perhaps the most crucial reason why salespeople make great leaders. They tend to have both a high degree of understanding and empathy that business is about people. All the studies won't amount to anything if you can't get others to come along with you on the journey. Salespeople know how to read others and connect with their inspirations and aspirations. They prioritise mutual understanding rather than focusing on points of difference and disagreement.

Though all employees of an organisation may have traits of a CEO, the following are some common attributes and requirements CEO's and salespeople share:

- **Committed and trustworthy:** Trust is never granted, it has to be won by sometimes admitting a weakness so that when they point out their solutions' strengths, those assertions have more value. The ability to earn trust or be perceived as someone who deserves that faith is an essential aspect of sales (and CEO) if they want people to follow them and gain confidence in their solutions and organisation.
- **Conviction**: Confidence is contagious, and salespeople learn the importance of enthusiasm early on. They naturally understand what's great about their products as they might even have created USP's for products and services they position in the market. CEOs that can transfer their enthusiasm to teams and customers have a significant advantage over the competition.
- **Creativity**: Salespeople always look for innovative ways to get in touch with a prospect or to win a deal. They aren't constrained by gatekeepers or objections and are usually on the lookout to solve a pressing customer's problem. A CEO has to do this at a scale and are compelled to think outside the box.
- **Customer-centric**: Salespeople perceive customers as the entity that finally pays their salary. To improve the customer experience as well as close new deals, salespeople have to think customer-centric when doing business. Without that, even the best technology, team, or organisational strategy won't lead

to business success.

- **Demand creation**: As a salesperson's career evolves, they equip themselves with expertise and competencies to create a market demand from scratch. Though demand creation is considered a team effort, the final USP design of a new product market entrance done by salespeople can reap high results. The salesperson has a better understanding on how to build rapport and discover the real needs. It's easier for them to decode the neurological fundamentals of a buyer's decision and advertise effectively.
- **Performance**: Sales, like leadership, is easy to feel worn out. Keeping an organisation moving requires constant attention and limitless energy always to push. Chasing leads, closing deals, and achieving quotas are skills salespeople learn that sets them up for a future of successful leadership performance.
- **Goal-driven**: The salesperson lives to achieve their KPIs, so goals and what it's going to take to complete them are always at the top of their mind. You can't run a successful organisation without KPIs, and CEOs who are conditioned salespeople are inherently goal-driven.
- **Have thick skin:** Salespeople deal with rejection daily, and they understand that it's merely part of their job to overcome serious obstacles to achieve success in any marketplace. Rejection can stop the most transformative concepts if the person leading the transformation can't deal with rejections properly. CEOs understand this concept and keep pushing, no matter the perceived odds.
- **Integrity**: Integrity is a core trait of salespeople. They know when they do something dishonest or unethical, and they will be exposed, this lousy reputation will ruin future sales prospects and the organisation's reputation. Both the CEO and the salesperson must prove their value by consistently acting with integrity.
- **Predictions**: Salespeople have to make forecast predictions of their sales targets constantly. They consciously and deliberately make predictions. They set themselves up to learn how to identify and execute these targets rather than relying on a happening to notice things are unusual.
- **Realise the value of growth:** Salespeople are not static, and they are always on the lookout for the next ample opportunity. They focus on exceeding their sales objectives, growing their customer base and sales pipeline. By the time they have maximised their compensation, they tend to move onto new pastures.
- **Strategic thinkers:** In sales, numbers don't lie and to figure out how to achieve them requires a strategic type of thinking. They can put complex matters into context for everyone to understand. They map out long-term plans that deal with challenges as they arise, which is a critical part of leadership, and it's something salespeople execute well.

- **Stubbornness**: Stubbornness is another trait shared due to having experimented various best-practice sales methods that are set in their ways. This stubbornness helps when they start something from scratch; they have the mindset to pull it through.
- **They close deals:** The salesperson's ability to navigate multiple minefields and coordinate the entire sales cycles in which they bring everyone together to make a deal happen is fundamental to running a successful organisation. Salespeople who became CEOs are deal-makers, and rest assured that wherever there's a business opportunity, they will use their previous experience to make the deal happen.

So, whether you are now entering the job market or looking for a new career path, a sales profession may be the right move to consider and don't worry; the following chapters are loaded with tips and techniques for salespeople to grow their brand to leave a legacy behind.

Chapter 4

Sales versus Business Developers

There are several different roles to consider when entering the sales labour market. Each role has various parameters for success, skills, experience, and other distinctive requirements. Let's start by stating that one can be an inside salesperson, an outside salesperson, or a combination of both roles. Then, we'll dig deeper into the definitions of each, their differences, how they support each other, which role chronologically comes first, and what activities need to be your priority based on the stage your organisation is in today.

The degree of separation between the inside and outside salespersons' roles and responsibilities will vary from organisation to organisation. The same salesperson might do both internal and external sales activities in smaller organisations, while larger organisations may have an inside salesperson in tandem with an outside salesperson, in which the inside and outside salespeople are one team, and both roles have a joint sales revenue quota to achieve. They are both responsible for bringing in qualified leads to close deals by turning prospects into customers.

The inside sales role is all about transactions while the outside sales role is the act of defining and pursuing: what, where, how, and to whom your organisation should sell to tomorrow. Both roles make sure the business is running in the short-term and will survive and grow in the long-term. Both roles are about winning transactional product deals, retaining and developing the customer. At the same time, the outside salesperson's role also includes identifying pathways to qualify new business opportunities for future business growth. The outside salesperson spends more time at the customer's site and should focus on buyers in the awareness and consideration stage. Within their organisation, the outside salesperson will interact closely with the research & development team, marketing, and inside salespeople to ensure the development and commercialisation of the right, demand-driven products.

The inside salesperson plays a back-office and admin role who works primarily behind the scenes and takes care of the internal commercial details. They rarely visit the customer's site but instead interact with them via videotelephony, telephone or emails. Their responsibility is to retain and develop their assigned customer base and build a strong partnership. In recent years, there has been a significant shift in sales activity between inside and outside sales roles. The inside salespeople are considered more effective and efficient when used in tandem with neuromarketing campaign strategies. The inside salesperson has a dynamic role, capable of cutting time and costs from the organisation's budget. Regardless of the organisation's size, they always have a quota to attain. They help the outside salespeople perform their customer-facing roles in ways that enable them to close deals quicker and to ensure the best customer experience. The inside salesperson is complementary to the outside salesperson, and their duties can include but not limited to:

- Maintaining an agreed level of telephone contact with both existing and potential customers.
- Pro-actively seeks new business opportunities by targeting a combination of both existing and potential customers.
- Routing qualified leads to external salespeople for further qualification and closure. They may also set up meetings for the outside salesperson.
- Effectively dealing with enquiries on invoicing, delivery status, product information and escalations with an agreed-upon response/reaction time.
- Assisting during tenders in gathering adequate information to ensure a successful tender submission. To note, though is that salespeople tend to proactively evaluate ways to engage much earlier in the sales cycle, well before the customer fully recognises what they want. Naturally, if you're going to win a deal, you have to get ahead of the RFP – thought research shows that, while getting ahead of the RFP is essential, it's no longer necessary since the most significant factor might be some sign that a prospect might not even be the right fit for an organisation's long-term strategy.
- Creating proposals and ensuring quotations are followed up to win the sales and increase the close ratio.
- Maximising sales growth by expanding their cross-sell and up-sell activities, thus establishing a healthy sales pipeline of business leads.
- Ensuring their external salesperson is updated on any escalations or other developments relevant to their assigned customer accounts.
- Maintains and creates customer profiles in the CRM tool, analyses data on performance and creates reports and analysis to interpret important data.

Having discussed some differences between inside and outside sales roles, we will now look at the different outside sales titles with their respective roles and responsibilities. Since each organisation has its unique methods to acquire, retain and develop customers, I'll shortly describe the titles in which I have gained experience over two decades:

<u>Sales Representative (Sales Rep):</u> It can be considered an entry point to the sales labour market, and like all sales roles, the sales rep has a quota to achieve. Though the sales reps primary function is to acquire new business through cold-calling and

door-to-door sales activities, they can be responsible for both inside and outside sales activities for customer acquisitions and retention.

Account Manager (or Account Executive): The account manager role can be considered a promotion from a sales representative role. Just like the sales rep, this position can be a combination of inside and outside sales activities, but traditionally, being an account manager involves having face-to-face meetings with customers, meaning you need support from an inside salesperson. Though the account manager is considered an outside role, you are responsible for developing existing customers and establishing new ones. Typically, you will spend time both at the customer's site and in your office doing admin work. The account manager evaluates creative approaches and innovative techniques to sell their organisation's solutions to meet their existing customer's needs. The goal of an account manager is customer retention and development for the long-term. Like all sales roles, the account manager brings in new business opportunities for the organisation through various sales methods, ranging from calling customers or face-to-face activities. To be successful in both the inside and outside sales roles, you should consistently bring in new sales leads and prospective customers to the organisation. It would help if you were self-motivated and goal-oriented to meet individual deadlines with little to no supervision, including prioritising your time and activities since it's somewhat both an inside and an outside sales role with potentially no internal sales support.

Key Account Manager (KAM): The KAM is mainly an outside sales role. This role is similar to the account manager role with the main difference being the word "key", meaning you are now assigned to a specific key customer segment to focus your work on with support coming from an internal salesperson. In comparison, an account manager might be assigned to the organisation's entire customer base, whereas the KAM is assigned to a specific key customer segment. Though being a KAM (like any other sales role) doesn't guarantee that the organisation has allocated resources for an internal salesperson, in this scenario, one must still be prepared to ask their manager why these critical success factors are missing. Because if such a vital success factor is absent, how can account planning (see Chapter 13) be implemented for the salesperson to increase the SOW on top customers?

Global Account Manager (GAM): The GAM is mainly an external and remote role that works primarily in large organisations where they regularly submit global tenders. They may have similar activities as the account manager and KAM with the difference being the word "Global", meaning they are assigned to a specific set of global (or Fortune 500) customers. The GAM works on global contracts in which customers can purchase a specific product globally for a fixed agreed-upon price. They usually work in tandem with a regional account manager, internal salesperson and other departments in order to address customer challenges and ensure a successful rollout of the global contract. Many large organisations have teams of staff who work on tenders to ensure the organisation wins business. In contrast, smaller organisations may leave tenders submissions to the salespeople who collaborate with different departments of their organisation to ensure a successful tender submission. Without internal support to ensure a successful rollout of the global contract or support from a team of staff who work on tender submissions, the GAM will have difficulties winning global contracts.

Business Development Managers (BDM): More emphasis is given to the BDM role due to it, in my opinion, being the most critical of all sales roles. The BDM role may combine outside and inside sales activities and often comes with a sales revenue quota. The BDM role is the most challenging of all sales roles, but it can also be the most gratifying role of all sales roles. The buyer's journey is where business development ends and sales begins. It passes through awareness, consideration, and selection phase: during the awareness phase, the buyer identifies their challenges and evaluates the different approaches or methods available to solve it. The consideration stage is where the buyer gets different options to select from, and they start filtering out options they don't want. In the selection stage, the customer identifies and buys into an opportunity they wish to pursue, and it's considered a top priority.

Job title aside, it's the focus on specific activities that makes the real difference between the BDM role and the other sales roles. Therefore, it is not surprising that salespeople are often confused with BDMs. Much of this is because too many organisations cloud the titles on purpose. There is still much confusion around its significance. Everyone has had some annoying experience with sales when the cold caller pushes you to your limit. Annoying experience comes about when the "hunter" type salesperson only shows attentiveness in closing the deal. Even when the customer isn't interested in whatever solution they are selling. This may be one reason why many organisations decided to rebrand the position from sales to BDM. Not only is every organisation unique in the way they use different titles and the tasks associated with these titles, but the BDM title sounds less threatening, so it can be easier to make calls and get appointments with prospects while using it. Ultimately, these titles are all different ways to refer to the same activity, which is getting your products into your customer's hands through various activities. However, it misleads people when you call yourself a BDM when, in fact, you plan to close a new business deal at the end of your customer interaction. Sales and BDM should not be considered the same role. Instead, think of them as two functions that are complementary to each other.

The degree of separation between these roles will vary from organisation to organisation. Especially in smaller organisations, people with sales titles may be involved in business development activities due to scarcity of resources. It's worth noting though that for a customer to become loyal, they might not realise many salespeople work with the customer's best interest in mind. Salespeople understand only a happy customer is a loyal customer that can generate significant recurring revenues gains while also achieving their sales quotas. Only a few actually behave like many people's image of the "pushy salesperson" today. Professional salespeople who seek out customers ready for change, challenge their status quo with provocative insights and advise them on how to buy best is still indispensable for many organisations.

The two primary reasons the sales engagement process is split into business development and sales is (i) the advantages of customisation and (ii) the increasing difficulty of reaching buyers. Customisation is widely regarded as a global trend, and since identifying a buyer today requires research and several touchpoints to connect, this has made it more concerning for the BDM to have a quota on their shoulder. However, this entirely depends on each organisation's strategy to have a sales and business developer structure. Organisations that split their sales cycle and engagement process into specific areas of responsibility maximise productivity and outcomes. Business development is relationship-building and is complementary to the sales and marketing teams, making it a standalone full-time position on any sales team. Therefore, less value gets added when the BDM has to shift gears between prospecting and closing deals. Beyond just improving the experience of lead generation, it takes time to adequately research prospects and qualify them, not to mention all the additional touchpoints required to capture a prospect's attention.

BDMs sit between the sales and the marketing ends of a continuum of functions through which a business penetrates a market and drives revenue growth. It's easy to see how important it is for both salespeople's and BDMs' strategies to work in tandem. An effective business development strategy isn't possible without a dedicated BDM, and relationships can only prosper if an organisation has products to offer and a reputation for being able to meet specific market demands with adequate resources. Hence, successful salespeople and BDMs have adequate resources they need to do their job along with a good predictive-drive that inspires them to achieve their sales goals—even to overachieve them.

When marketing material is available, and target customers are defined to whom you sell what your organisation can deliver today, then you are in sales. When your focus is on defining or pursuing what, where, how, and to whom your organisation should sell tomorrow, then you are a BDM. For salespeople to close more deals in a financial year, the BDM's strategy should shorten the product go-to-market phase and enhance the sales engagement process to shorten the sales cycle. The interaction approach with customers can be defined as the BDM creates long-term value through innovation and technology, while salespeople share information about their products portfolio and advise customers to close the sale. Salespeople are entirely concerned in winning deals with the qualified leads coming from the BDM. These are initiatives done in the product time-to-market phase or during new product launches and marketing campaigns. The BDM brings in enough qualified leads to generate a certain amount of revenue, but in some instances, closing the sale and turning leads into customers is beyond their direct control. Sales is all about closing, and they take the deal to the finish line after they have received a qualified lead from the BDM. The core functions of a BDM haven't changed much in recent years, but the process of prospecting and qualifying leads has a new meaning.

In other words, BDMs approach the market with an exploring and learning mindset to uncover and capture challenges that their organisation's technological capabilities can address. Like all sales roles, the BDM shares direct customer feedback and works with the research and development team to develop a fitting product addressing the customer's challenge that are aligned with the salesperson's long-term organisational business strategy. The BDM gathers business intelligence, conducts research and defines activities to develop a pipeline of prospective leads. Once these well-qualified leads are generated, the BDM hands them over to the sales team for further vetting and closing and if necessary to negotiate the contract terms.

Much has changed in the way we qualify leads, and the proliferation of conversational sales and marketing tools are proof of this dramatic shift. Your customer's time is valuable, and giving them the ability to control when and how they interact with you is challenging. When you waste your customer's time, you will annoy them, and they will begin to associate your brand with feeling irritated. Salespeople realise that selling is a time and numbers game and the only way to recover from rejections and failures is to predict optimism and pick up the phone (or get back into your email) and keep reaching out. Also, having the right tools, systems, processes and good governance will keep salespeople on track and help win additional time.

There is no substitute for emailing your leads, making cold calls, and having conversations with existing customers, or potential prospects. Learn from every interaction to develop an understanding of what motivates your customers to buy or not buy. Your number one competitor today is the customer's status quo, that is, what your customer is doing right now. If you understand that, you will have a much easier time providing customers with something that adds value. Therefore, when hiring salespeople, look for traits that view their role as a partner for achieving a win-win situation. Selling is like artwork, yet not all artists can draw, nor do they all understand the colour codes. Even if the artist knows how to draw and uses the right colour codes, there is still little chance of becoming a recognised artist. That said, just because a salesperson has mastered every survival skill in the book. It doesn't mean they're going to develop partnerships that achieve a win-win situation to attain the customer for the long-term.

At this point, it's clear there are numerous different types of sales roles. Now, it's time to discuss the methods that determine sales success over failure. Salespeople might perform additional qualification activities in certain circumstances, but their primary objective is to win deals and meet or surpass their organisation's revenue and growth targets. That said, a productive business development strategy relies on an agile business model that we will discuss in the next chapter.

Chapter 5

Business Models are Sales Strategies

A business model is a structure of the business, and it explains how they operate, generate revenue, and how it intends to achieve its vision. A business model is a complementary element to the product features, benefits, and value an organisation delivers to its customers. It analyses a market segment's values, proposes products or services for that specific market segment, and shapes plans to enhance the business's capability and capacity to perform business activities within that market segment. Yet constant technological disruption is making business models more vulnerable today than ever before. Although almost all business models eventually become obsolete, confusion and misunderstanding still surround the concept of them - a concept that could become the basis of additional competitive advantage.

The demand shift in market segments and transformational initiatives in an organisational structure forces many organisations to continuously evaluate their processes and business models to ensure they are economically sustainable with enhancements in cutting-edge technology. They might also have to reverse prior business models and sales methods, even though they might have once been successful. Many business models have been created for specific market industry needs in the business-to-business (B2B) or business-to-consumer (B2C) sectors. The best business models and sales methodologies (or sales engagement process) are agile to change depending on the situation, and organisations will have different business models and sales methods at different phases of its maturity. Therefore, the business models and sales engagement process that works in one aspect of your organisation's growth may harm it at a different stage.

The critical part of the business model work is the implementation of a sales strategy in which the internal sales engagement process gets examined to improve customer experience and to increase the win-ratio. Changes to any part of the sales engagement process can be proactive or forced by the competition. However, these organisational initiatives may also happen due to the shift in customer demands or when technology creates transformational opportunities (or threats) to the existing business model.

The most challenging part of B2B sales today is not only that customer behaviour is changing, forcing salespeople to do things differently, but that customers don't need salespeople the way they did in the past. In previous decades, salespeople had become proficient at discovering the customers' need and positioning a solution for them which was generally a combination of components and services, who then explained how complicated it would be for the customer to implement it on their own. This worked quite well because customers didn't know how to solve their problems, even if they had an understanding of them. However, due to the increased procurement and purchasing services now available, including other outsourcing services, organisations can enthusiastically define their needs by themselves. They research and gathering data over the web and arrive at a deep understanding of what they need and present it in a well-scoped RFP. In this world, salespeople can be more of a nuisance than an advantage because businesses that deal with outsourcing are often way ahead of the salesperson.

Customers today expect more knowledgeable salespeople who provide advice that helps them make well-informed decisions. Whatever that decision may end up being, the salesperson should remain emotionally intuitive, organised, empathetic, and forward-thinking. One thing is sure: due to the ever-swifter evolution of innovation and technology, we will continue to see changes in the way we buy and sell, and traditional salespeople will find it increasingly difficult to keep up. Also, customers will continue to use publicly available information to assess their demands, and sometimes also turn to external virtual working teams or sophisticated purchasing consultants who help them secure the best possible deals from suppliers. Regardless of the sales title, business models or sales methodologies you use, every salesperson needs to find their journey to reach their desired peak. Certain core principles have worked again and again, at its core, the customer purchases for their reasons, not yours.

Conceptual B2B Sales (or Solution Selling)

The conceptual B2B sales process is formed out of the organisations business model. To explain where business development (generating revenue) fits into an organisation's business model, we describe this structure as conceptual B2B selling (or solution selling).

Conceptual B2B sales methods have transformed conventional sales thinking from the traditional product sales. Instead of product-led selling that focuses on specific features and functions, conceptual B2B sales are solution-led, connecting the sales cycle to the customers' demands while mapping their natural buying habits to your solution. Therefore, salespeople who are good in product sales might have it more challenging with conceptual B2B sales due to the combination of several different components and the various touchpoints and stages in the long sales cycle. Conceptual B2B sales is a broadly applied selling method that deals specifically with the selling of complex configurations combining components, products and services to deliver an end-to-end solution that solves the pressing customer problems.

Conceptual B2B selling is the genuine interest in learning and focuses on understanding a customers' challenge; it seeks to identify discrepancies and root causes on what they need to accomplish and how they measure success, thus helping a salesperson then tailor recommendations and options. Conceptual B2B selling is a consultative selling approach where the customer and salesperson work together to identify needs that lead to a concept (or solution) to solve a customers' challenge or be adaptive, offering minor or incremental changes to an existing system.

Selling products (not solutions) involves marketing products one at a time, whereas conceptual B2B sales are multiple components coming together to form an end-to-end solution. For purposes of illustrating the difference between a product and solution, I will use the term product to refer to goods and services, as well as for offerings that include the two. For example, let's take a skilled carpenter (a service) who has a hammer (a product) and a nail (another product) when hitting the nail head with the hammer, the hammer becomes part of the solution for hanging a picture on the wall, or for building a bridge, or for even developing a commercial real estate building. In other words, a product does something simple, whereas a solution solves a specific need.

The conceptual B2B sales method is a validated engagement process that has shown to deliver significant and consistent increases in revenue. In the conventional solution-sales methodology that has prevailed since the 1980s, salespeople demonstrated why their solution is better than its competition. This process continues, but salespeople now align their solutions with a deep understanding of the customers' needs by asking clarification questions before demonstrating why their solution is the best fit. In essence, there are two types of clarification questions:

(i) Closed questions mean the customer can only answer with yes or no. An example of a closed question can be, *"Will you make the decision this month?"* This closed question leaves little room for the customer to elaborate further where they would usually respond with a yes or no answer.

(ii) Open questions begin with how, who, what, when, where, and why enables the customer to elaborate further. The same example with an open question can be, *"When will you make the decision?"* Here the customer may need to elaborate further allowing the salesperson to dig even deeper.

In both product sales and conceptual B2B selling, salespeople focus on controlling the relationship at a process level on how the work gets done, not necessarily at a subconscious level around feelings, behaviours of someone or who finally does the work. In both product sales and conceptual B2B sales, the customer first searches the web before deciding to purchase a product or to contact the manufacture to learn more. By now, the customer is willingly ready to work with the salesperson who offers advice on the best return of investment for an end-to-end conceptual B2B solution.

The conceptual B2B sales methodology ultimately boils down to three phases: (i) assess and qualify information gathered, (ii) provide adequate information, and (iii) gain the customer's acceptance. Trading qualitative information builds the buyer's trust as they join you in consultative discussions. You can engage with buyers more efficiently and position your values appropriately to close the deal. Conceptual B2B sales rely on an ongoing transfer of knowledge and information between a buyer and a salesperson. Essentially, if your interactions involve exchanging large amounts of information and data for the customer to make a well-informed decision, then you are a salesperson selling conceptual B2B solutions.

When discussing conceptual B2B sales, we refer to a different approach than transactional selling of products and services. The separation of these two approaches also depends on the customers purchasing process. For example, when a customer plans to purchase and install a new visual communication system, they can either submit a public tender or directly enter into a contractual agreement with their preferred supplier, in which the supplier submits to the customer a full-scope solution offering and the negotiations begin. Even though tenders may be considered mandatory by law, some entities may bypass this process due to financial and staff capacity restraints within their organisation or when the new visual communication system has a low estimated value or even when the entity is pleased with their incumbent-supplier and see no need for a tender. Let's take a scenario where an entity doesn't submit a public tender, and the salesperson is in the process of qualifying the visual communication (or Digital Signage) opportunity. Whichever approach finally applies, both the entity and the salesperson should consider discussing amongst others some of the following factors in scope, time, and costs:

Scope (Deliverables/Inclusions/Exclusions)

The scope will encompass all that is included and excluded in sale. It describes the benefits, the work required, and the results it's intended to achieve. For the prospect to understand and accept the scope, the salesperson first needs to define the scope and its limits with the customer by considering:

- The business objective of the visual communication solution: (i) The prospect needs to ask themselves what is their objective with the digital signage solution? Is it to drive sales, to enhance brand awareness, to educate and inform, to create a more sophisticated customer experience, to reduce marketing printing costs, to monetise screens, a combination of all of the above, or for something else? (ii) Who is the audience? Are they usual customers, visitors, employees, volunteers, or other viewers? (iii) How do they measure ROI performance? Is it going to be audience demographics gathered in real-time, will the sales data be linked to the time when specific content is showing, will the solution be using social media or other analytics tools?

- Content (is King): (i) What content will be displayed on the visual communication solution? (ii) Where do they see the usage of their visual communication content? In restaurants (cafeteria or for menus), as a wayfinding/navigation system, for emergency notifications, for third party advertisements (monetising), for queue management, for self-registration, for information announcements, for news/entertainment/sports. (iii) What content type will be used? PowerPoint slides, Adobe, QR Codes/Tags, Audio, 3D content, HD images/video, 4K images/video, Live feeds, RSS feeds, Internal database (e.g. events, calendar, menu, etc.), External database (e.g. social media, traffic, weather, local news, etc.), Animation graphics, Static images (JPEG or PNG), Split-screen, Interactive media (touch-screen), change content by location or time.
- The Hardware: Now that we have understood their business objective and content sources, we want to understand the hardware scope. Based on the business objective; (i) How many locations will have the visual communication solution installed? (ii) Where do they intend to install the solutions? Will it be also in a vehicle (bus, train or others), at a Bus/Train Station, or in the middle of town? (iii) Will they be installed as a floor-standing (poster-like stand) solution, will the screen be hanging from the ceiling, will they require a ceiling-mount fixture or wall-mount fixture? (iv) Do they require an indoor or outdoor screen or do they need a high brightness display, and will the screen require a 24/7 runtime? (v) Will the visual communication solution be a video wall, an interactive kiosk, or will the screen be entirely embedded in another device like a vending machine? (vi) What level of interactivity is required? (vii) Will it be a one-way broadcast stream of information with no touchscreen interactivity? (viii) Will it be an interactive touchscreen with single or multi-touch points? (ix) Will it be a touchless interactivity screen with gesture-based controls?
- The Software: (i) Will the CMS (Content Management System) be centrally managed at one location, or will it be a web-based (decentralised) management from multiple sites? (ii) Will it be a cloud-based (SaaS) CMS software that is hosted and communicates with an onsite media player via an internet connection? (iii) Will it be an on premises-based CMS software installed on a server where your server pushes content onto the screen? (iv) Should content get triggered by age/gender/race of the viewer? (v) Will the solution require a media player embedded into the screen? (vi) Will the media player be for Android or Windows-based devices?
- Quality: What level of quality must the deliverables have? It is important to note that quality standards mean different things to different people. Though quality can be described as a separate element to the scope; quality is by

default also linked with an end-users perception of quality, meaning your organisation will ensure it upholds quality standards accordingly. For example, the quality standard could include product standardisation that is not required for smaller organisations who prefer the latest technology. In contrast, the global customer (or Fortune 500 organisations) requires product standardisation and product stability to be able to purchase the same product (and components) for several years to reduce maintenance costs. In this scenario, an import element for the global customer (or Fortune 500 organisations) is PLM (product lifecycle management) and product transitions. In providing global customers with this information, they can better prepare their annual purchase and rollouts.

- The Services (or resources): (i) What type of support and services is required? (ii) How do they plan to create content? (iii) Will the prospect use in-house resources, will they hire an external agency, will they acquire ready-made content, will they rely on the screen manufacturer to create content, or do they have other content resources? (iv) What support or installation services are required? (v) Does the prospect require an assessment onsite, project management, creative services, training, technical and ongoing support? (vi) Is a service level agreement (SLA) required to ensure high uptime availability, or will the customer take care of the maintenance and reparations themselves?

Timeframe (Schedules)

Though time is the services (or resources) already described in scope that includes all requirements of the specified services to achieve the end result, the time required to produce and deliver the goods and services is described here.

When you qualify a business lead, it will help if you had an understanding of:

- When does the customer plan to see results with the new environment?
- What is the timeframe (e.g. 3, 6, 9, 12 months) for completing the installation?
- Do they at least have a deadline to when they would likely make the purchase order?

Salespeople usually follow the same chronological approach in the lead generation and qualification phase. Though the following are not direct elements of time, they are definite prerequisites your prospect should have to intellectually and emotionally agree on before they can make a confident decision to invest time in you or your organisation. Therefore, it would be extremely helpful to get an understanding of them:

- Business opportunity qualification: Interview the decision-makers around their beliefs and interest in the business opportunity and try to identify other challenges and any future business priorities.

- The priority of the subject matter: What priority level does this potential business opportunity have within their organisation over other important matters, and what pressing issue is the solution intended to solve?
- Effect: What evidence can the prospect provide in dollar values that prove the existence of a problem, and how will they know when they have solved it, and how do those issues tie into the bigger picture the organisation is attempting to solve?
- Organisational context: You need to understand what your prospect is trying to solve in a broader context. Also, you want to discover what might have stopped their organisation from addressing these issues on their own?
- Restrictions (or lessons learned): If specific problems are not addressed upfront, these may have been the same factors that hindered the prospect's organisation in the past that may hinder them again in the future. Have these issues been adequately addressed?
- Resources: What is each sponsors' or stakeholders' thought and views on their appropriate investment of time, people and money?
- Decision-making criteria: What decision-making criteria applies for each sponsor or stakeholder that would allow them to make a well-informed decision whether the prospect selects you or someone else? What would each sponsor have to believe or experience before they would give you their vote?

Sales jobs can be the highest paid role in an organisation, so your time is one of the most valuable assets of your organisation. Therefore, your goal is to be efficient and economical as possible with your time. That said, for SME organisations, you will need to know who the decision-makers are while for larger organisations, you will additionally need to understand their decision-making process as described later in chapter 14 (Sales Engagement Preparation Plan).

In order to make the most out of each customer interaction, it's essential not only to see prospects and talk to them but to use the right tactics and tools to ensure future interactions. For instance, during the first meeting with your prospect, set up a second meeting date, rather than waiting until later to do this. By being proactive, you can shorten the sales cycle by a couple of weeks. The longer the sales cycle, the less likely the sale will happen because it suggests this opportunity might not be a priority to your prospect. This is just one example of how timing becomes a vital success factor in closing more new deals per annum.

Depending on the solution you are selling and other factors, the sales cycle can take as long as four months or even ten to close the deal. The appointment you make today will create the prospect you meet tomorrow, the sales presentation you make next week, and so on, ultimately leading to the closing of the sale. Any engagement cycle has one primary goal, which is to shorten the sequence of something. If you can close a deal in half the time you used to, you can close twice as many in the same period. For that reason, when a salesperson qualifies a good lead and acquires knowledge of the prospects decision-making process, their deadlines and budget planning, this will enable the salesperson to add leverage to drive urgency in the sales cycle. When examining the entire sales cycle, from the prospect qualification phase up to receipt of the PO (purchase order), you can see why the concept of time is so important. The idea of time, for a salesperson, also means shortening the sales cycle by prioritising activities that bring quick wins while also achieving long-term impact on customer experience.

Costs (Budget)

Salespeople can either get insights around the customers budget when the scope has been defined or by asking questions around their estimated budget per visual communication installation, their estimated budget for this business need or their annual IT/ICT organisational budget.

Through experience, salespeople have learned that not all customers are willing to share sensitive information about their budget for a specific business need. Still, if you don't ask, the answer will always be no.

The advent of conceptual B2B sales has an impact on business models and operational excellence. The success of conceptual B2B sales depends on the salesperson's attitude and commitment to learning but also on the organisation's tools, processes, policies and practices. Sales professionals witness success over failure and use this understanding and best practice method in assessing every following job on which business models and sales engagement processes are either successful or rarely work.

PART II - Due Diligence

"We all strive to get along and accept our differences, not necessarily agree on them – by understanding and appreciating perspectives of others is the willingness to learn."

Chapter 6

Pre-Sales Phase of the Sales Cycle

In this and the following chapter, we will discuss the two separate phases of the sales cycle: pre-sales and post-sales. The Pre-sales phase has three milestones and is a set of sales activities (or a process) done before selling a product or solution. The post-sales phase discussed in the following chapter has two milestones in which the contract gets awarded, and the operational activities begin with the delivery of the goods and the final installation.

Every business operates according to its own set of rules, and there is no one-size-fits-all solution when it comes to finding the best sales cycle approach (or sales engagement process). There are numerous sales cycles and engagement processes in the marketplace that derive real value. However, whatever the specific methods, the sales cycle usually follows the same five-milestones described in these two chapters.

Many sales leaders prefer a particular sales cycle because it comes naturally to them and fits their unique style. However, first and foremost, the chosen sales cycle should reflect the buyer's journey. To avoid missing business opportunities, take the time to learn what motivates your buyer to buy and tailor each customers' sales experience by determining the customers' social style that we will discuss later in chapter 9 (Archetypes In Perspective). As you research and collect clues in your interactions with a customer (or prospect), you will find insights into their behaviour and preferences.

Mastering each stage of the five milestone in the sales cycle is essential to sales performance success. If you or your organisation is weak in one or more milestone areas, you won't thrive, so identifying weak points and continuing to make progress on them is vital to improving sales results. There are also many critical success factors out of the salesperson's control that might be dysfunctional or where vital inputs are missing. Naturally, this prolongs the sales cycle and can even lead to completely losing the deal, through no fault of the salesperson. We will discuss the factors out of the salesperson's control later in chapter 11 (Source Of Power In B2B Sales) and 12 (Strategic Organisational Capabilities).

Five Milestones of the Sales Cycle

A strong understanding of the sales cycle and engagement process helps salespeople improve the management of factors they can control to grow their win ratio. No matter what B2B solution you sell, every sale follows roughly the same five milestone pattern:

- Milestone 1 - Lead Generation and Qualification is where you build rapport with the customer on their demand.
- Milestone 2 - Position Your Product or Solution is where you develop your Unique Selling Proposition (USP).
- Milestone 3 - Negotiations and getting the customers' commitment is where you present your proposal (and USP). You also elaborate on the customer's objections and concerns about your organisation or your solution, meeting their demand.
- Milestone 4 - Won the deal is where the contract is awarded. If the deal is lost, this is where you can now interview the customer to learn the reason for losing.
- Milestone 5 - Delivery and implementation. This is where the organisations' operational excellence delivers goods timely, in a flawless condition, and the installation is successful. Also, this is where the salesperson now begins to retain and develop the customer further by restarting the entire milestone process again.

The following illustration of the five milestones in the sales cycle presents the sales cycle's chronology and sales engagement process. As mentioned, pre-sales are all the activities found in milestone 1, 2, and 3 of the sales cycle and is the end product of exhaustive research and development.

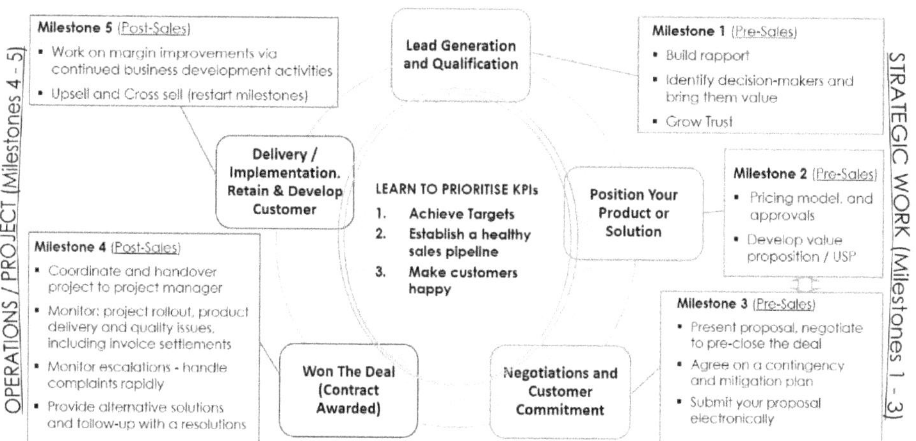

Milestone # 1 – Generate and Qualify Leads

Lead qualification is a process of sales and marketing collaborating to forecast the likelihood that a prospect will ultimately purchase. It occurs at every stage of the sales cycle and eventually dictates if the prospect will be funnelled down the sales pipeline.

If you are assigned to public customers, you could join one of the several electronic platforms shared by the federal government, cantons, and communes for public procurement purposes that offer a simple procedure for public contract-awarding authorities to post their tenders and any other relevant tender documents. The same applies if you are assigned to private customers which we call Intertrading. Intertrading is a term that indicates business transactions being a two-way street, featuring both Private Tender Opportunities and B2B-specific leads. Like for public customers, Intertrading aims to ensure procurement and tenders are easily managed and transparent.

In essence, qualifying a business lead is gathering the insights necessary to make good judgment to then prioritise your time and effort. In my opinion, qualifying leads is somewhat like being an archaeologist digging an ancient city out of the ground. You might have a few traces about where the city is buried, but you don't quite know what it will resemble until it's unearthed. Most excavations start with solid research, such as gathering information from archives and other sources. This helps the archaeologist understand what they are looking for, as well as where it might be found. The next step is surveying the area with techniques like remote sensing or direct visual observation. After archaeologists have thoroughly studied the site, only then do they begin digging. They dig small holes to determine the location, density and spread of artefacts. The archaeologists proceed with excavating the site using various tools. They remove dirt and document the precise location of any artefacts that are found. The background of the artefact is just as important as the artefact itself, so these findings are always thoroughly mapped and documented. The dirt removed from the site is sifted through a screen to search for small artefacts that may have been unnoticed during the initial excavation. After the archaeologists have excavated the site accordingly, they fill the excavation site back in and take the artefacts to be analysed at a lab, either locally or at the archaeologist's home institution. They are examined and classified based on the research questions put forth by the archaeologist. The artefacts are grouped with other artefacts of the same type, and this depends on a variety of characteristics such as features or style. Archaeologists also try to determine how old artefacts are. One way this can be done is relative to other artefacts using stratigraphy – the idea that older artefacts are found in the earth below newer ones.

Salespeople don't dig in the dirt, but like archaeologists, they research to understand what they're looking for and where to proceed. Like when the archaeologist digs an ancient city out of clay (sometimes they may have a surprise), a salesperson might have clues about where to find a potential prospect, but they don't quite know what the business opportunity will look like until it gets qualified (salespeople too will be rewarded with a surprise). Solid research helps salespeople understand what they are looking for, as well as where a business opportunity might be found. What the surveying, digging, excavating, classifying and grouping the artefacts is for the archaeologists, so is the lessons-learned, research, preparation, segmentation, qualification, and archiving information in the CRM tool is for the salespeople.

Qualifying leads and closing deals requires salespeople to determine several variables. Often, these variables are qualified in the early stages of the sales cycle, because many customers don't give salespeople the time of day unless there is a clear and present need. If you are lucky, you might have called at the right time when the customer has a demand for the products you sell, but this is rarely the case. Relying on luck will hurt your sales performance on several levels. Instead, cultivating sales leads and managing the entire sales cycle demands a disciplined and agile planning approach.

The way you qualify business leads will affect sales performance in a significant way. Filtering through leads can become an expensive undertaking because, for salespeople, wasted time equals missed business opportunities and revenue streams from elsewhere. So, if you don't have the right qualification process upfront, pursuing a constant flood of leads will do more harm than good, and where the prospect has no real priority on a given need, there will be no purchase. Through techniques and tips described in this book, including one's lessons-learned while working in an organisation will help salespeople discover how to qualify a lead properly.

However, all too often inexperienced salespeople jump to the positioning stage too quickly, without first gaining a proper understanding of the customer's environment and desires. If you are: not qualifying your leads efficiently, or if you don't know who your high-value customers are, or if you don't know their decision-making process, you will waste time and energy chasing the wrong leads, attempting to sell to customers who might not even be a good fit for your organisation's overall strategy. Even worse, you might have identified an excellent fit but lose the deal because you aren't talking to the right decision-makers. Make sure you spend enough time on determining the customers who bring wins and who have the highest possibility of delivering substantial, valuable results for you and your organisation.

To achieve a more efficient lead qualification approach, focus on understanding basics like your prospect's competitors, key players, or who your prospect's end customers are before you can identify where your solutions map their needs. Though many qualification frameworks exist, B2B lead generation attributes of a qualified prospect should answer the following questions:

- Does the prospect have a genuine interest in what your company offers?
- Are you speaking to a decision making with the authority to purchase?
- Does the prospect have the finances and can they afford what you sell?
- When does the prospect plan to see results?

If you are genuinely committed to becoming a salesperson and have enough fire on your own, you will make sales no matter what you do. Still, if you don't develop a strategy and keep things documented, or don't keep analysing and adjusting your approach, you will not shorten the sales cycle nor improve your close ratio over time.

Determining the customer's precise business need is all about asking the right questions to the right people. Whether your prospect has an open-door policy or not, your goal has to be to get the appointment. The setting of the first appointment does not necessarily mean you are dealing with a potential customer. It merely means you are dealing with a lead, prospect, or candidate to build rapport.

Milestone # 2 – Product Positioning

Sales and business development roles are in constant transformation. They may still be positioning solutions, but broadly, they will be selling awareness. An example of selling awareness is, for instance, when talking about cancer as a major disease affecting thousands of individuals. This makes the topic a very emotional one for many people. Therefore, the advertisement campaign should have an overall forceful message that appeals to the need to aggress in readers. The advertisement reaches out to those who are enraged at cancer and want to destroy it rather than treating it. This aggressive tone can also be seen in the colour coding selected such as red, orange and yellow. Depending on the region, these colours evoke a sense of anger that helps pursue an aggressive bias towards cancer. After getting the reader fired up towards their cause, this aggression brings urgency that is addressed by the unique selling proposition (USP) of the advertisement. This overall tone becomes effective towards pulling in readers by appealing to strong, natural reactions. This makes the difference between a marketing campaign that goes nowhere and one that ensures progress.

USP (unique selling proposition) is usually what an organisation thinks its strength and uniqueness are, whereas positioning is what the organisations' target audience think about them. By identifying and communicating the organisation's compelling offer and benefits, the USP should answer the customer's question, What's in it for me? For example, McDonald's USP is that their food taste is consistent no matter where you go in the world, a Big Mac always taste like a Big Mac.

Where competition is intense, it becomes even more critical to get your product positioning right, every time. One way to do this is to consider your customer's motives. Salespeople can be regarded as neuromarketers that gain customer insight into their preferences and decision motivators. They can be helpful in product development and to form creative advertising campaigns for the target audience. However, one should remember that no matter how great you think your product or solution may be, it has no significant value until the customer agrees that it also looks good for them. Products and services derive value, so if there is no pressing issue, the product will address or relevant results the client can expect from it, then the product will not be compelling.

Product positioning is an integral part of a sales and marketing strategy. It's determined by customer segments and their needs. Product positioning helps the target audience understand what value a product offers (including the return on investment for the money paid for it) and how it compares with competing products. Along with defining product benefits, segmentation, and determining customer needs, another critical element of product positioning is credibility, just as an essential aspect of cultivating prospects is trust.

Product positioning is never about you, your products, or your organisation. Your product or solutions have no inherent value; they derive value from challenges people intend to solve that they care about or a result, people want to produce that they highly value. For a product or solution to be meaningful, it has to address something important whereas, for credibility, there should be some evidence of how the problem evolved and how the customer will measure and know when a solution solved their pressing problem. Since there may be many problems your customer or prospect faces, you should get a complete list of all of them and get a sense of priority. You want to understand what the customer is attempting to solve in a broader context (as explained with the nail and the hammer). You also want to explore what had hindered their organisation in the past might hinder them again if issues are not addressed adequately.

It's critical to take the time to master the ability to not talk about your product or solution in an initial customer conversation. It is a critical step to change the dynamics of the initial customer conversations from a pattern of "tell, assume, guess," to a dialogue of mutual exploration and hopefully mutual understanding. When relationship building is done well, the rest of the opportunity conversation should roll out logically and naturally. If you decide not to take this approach, you will spend much of your time only speaking about your product or solution. The customer will ask you questions about your products or services, and you will respond. By the end of the conversation, you will have little understanding of what is important and of interest to the customer.

The objective of refraining from talking about your solution is to have the customer to start talking about the problem and the outcome they hope to produce. It's helpful to set clear expectations by gaining the customer's permission for you to ask questions because you want first to understand someone before they can understand you. As you learn to manoeuvre the conversation when the customer wants to discuss features and functions around your products, you focus on getting a list of the customer's constraints and pressing issues they want to solve. Once you have the list of the pressing issues, get their insights on which issue is higher weighted over the others and why is that the case because you can't help a customer succeed who doesn't understand their perceived need. After you have understood their constraints and pressing issues according to their prioritisation, you can now enter the discussion of their internal decision-making process because you cannot help a customer succeed if they cannot decide. At a given point, you should have gained a better understanding of the customer's situation to at least have one powerful option when addressing the elements of value in your UPS (unique selling proposition).

When you avoid positioning your product, there are some helpful hints to keep in mind. If a customer asks you to talk about your products or services, answer their questions by using this guideline: make a short statement to the customer around their required outcome within the context of their overall business. For example, you could say, "Sure, I will be glad to see how we can help. You know, I've done some research and learned why customers choose to work with us, which leads me to believe that what we do can deliver some significant benefits to your organisation. I was hoping to ask you some questions to eliminate any guesswork upfront". After you have stated this, observe their reaction (or body language) before you give a brief explanation for your request. You could then say something like, "Is it okay if I ask you a few questions to be sure I understand what is important to your organisation and completely address what you want to accomplish?". Remember to use some of the customer's exact words in your responses and questions the customer used themselves. When doing this, you literally speak their language and demonstrate how well you listen and how attentive you are to what they want. However, when controlling your language down to the customer's exact words, be careful of using the word BUT. Instead, end the sentence instantly or use AND because using the word but in a sentence can negate everything that came before it. For example, you could instead say, "That's a good question; could you help me get a better understanding here?"

Knowing what is essential to your customer is imperative to properly prepare product positioning. Admittedly, this is not always easy – some customers you speak with may not understand their organisation's real challenges, or they are too overwhelmed with its complexity to examine the big picture and identify fundamental changes for improvements. Yet when you can show your customer that you have done your research, you've spoken to many people from different parts of their organisation, and you've shared references of how you helped other organisations in similar situations. This shows you know the customer's situation that they might not even be aware of, thus illustrating you are an advisor providing the customer options to achieve a higher return on investments when working with you. This approach establishes credibility to create long-term loyalty with the target audiences. It builds the customer's trust in you as you discuss the customer purchase journey's and mapping process, not your selling journey.

Let's now discuss the fundamental motivation to buy. It stems from three aspects of our environment: grievance, growth, and transformation (or transformative innovation - meaning creating business models that are profitable, competitive and long-lasting). We all wish to move away from grievance and move towards growth. Yet, grievance without growth is something everyone seeks to avoid. We demand less of the things we don't want and strive to be where we can achieve growth for peace of mind. Also, we usually pay attention to something new in our environment or transformative innovation that can shift entire systems over time making a new viable fit for the future that moves us away from the grievance or moves us towards growth. If your product or solution is disconnected, neither reducing grievance nor enabling growth, it's unlikely that the customer will spend time, effort, people, and money trying to learn more about it. This expenditure of resources could also be considered painful.

Establishing credibility as both a salesperson and a brand creates long-term loyalty with target audiences. People who trust a brand are more inclined to purchase it, so transparency and a clear tone are the best practices to promote effective product positioning. That is why marketers don't use high-pressure tactics or flowery language to demonstrate their product's value and benefits. When a product positioning feels natural and even modest, it can add massive value to your sales and marketing. Credibility is established by presenting evidence such as case studies, testimonials, customer reviews, or even product transitions strategies and product roadmaps. Also, inviting customers to events, workshops, and providing them with test units to evaluate are all convenient and effective for product positioning. Organisations usually invest some of their budgets in offering their salespeople access to such tools and techniques.

When done well, positioning helps a product succeed. When positioning is poorly done, even a high-quality product may fail. To make product positioning work, organisation isolate precisely what makes their product and brand unique. Remember, your value proposition must answer one crucial question: how will your product improve your customers' lives? Your target audience will dismiss your product if they don't see that it has much value to them. This makes the value proposition the riskiest aspect of product positioning, and one of the hardest to perform effectively. Examine the most valuable elements of your competitor's product positioning message compared to your own, and then look for ways to deliver on your organisation's value and the interests of each customer segment.

Note that customers want flexibility and usually don't like to be limited in their options when making a purchase decision. Giving them a range of options for their needs makes it more likely they will choose any one option from you. So whenever possible, rather than positioning a single option, submit a proposal with more than one option. Also, whenever possible, before submitting your proposal electronically, go on-site and present the proposal to the decision-makers in person to secure their commitment which we will now discuss in milestone three.

Milestone # 3 – Negotiations and Commitment

In milestone 3, we will discuss the negotiation preparation phase, not the negotiation process discussed later in chapter 8 (Build Rapport Before Negotiating).

As illustrated in chapter 2, when you are ill, and you visit your doctor to restore your health through the practice of medicine. Milestone 1 is where the doctor reviews information from the patient's history. In Milestone 2, the doctor examines the patient and identifies symptoms which the patient is experiencing. With the data from the patient's history and the identified symptoms, the doctor has enough information to decide whether to prescribe a medicine or healing therapy.

By now, you have invested much effort to make sure your presentation and USP is rooted in facts interpreted within the customer's business context that persuades them one way or the other to move forward with your organisation or to move in another direction with the competition. Though presenting the proposal is a crucial part of closing the deal, the most critical step in negotiating and influencing is to build rapport and earn the customer's commitment.

In negotiation and influence, we find it fascinating what is seen in the animal kingdom. The lion attempting to defend his territory from another male intruder will act with rigid vigilance and threatening or even combative behaviour. The rival male is not the trigger per se, but some specific characteristic about the intruder prompts this response. Usually, this trigger characteristic will be just one tiny aspect of the intruder's overall being - the sound of intruder's roar could have been the trigger. Humans too have these pre-programmed triggers. The same trigger features that work to our favour with one customer can be a disadvantage with another customer as we become used into playing the pre-programmed triggers at the wrong time. For instance, one customer may respond well to a bright smile and a question about their family, while another may be more reserved that finds this approach phoney, irrelevant, or a waste of time.

Though many negotiation preparation processes used today have shorter phases, success is still determined by what you do before you sit at the negotiation table. Therefore, before entering negotiations, there is the preparation and planning stage. The negotiating parties use this stage to determine the What? How? Who? Why? Where? When? and How much? questions with much clarity.

Chapter 7

Post-Sales Phase of the Sales Cycle

In this chapter, we will describe the remaining two (of the five milestones) post-sales milestones of the sales cycle.

No matter how simple or complex the B2B concept, the entire sales cycle and engagement process relies on the integration of a multidisciplinary approach. The salesperson requires support from other parts of the organisation to help in the pre-sales phase (chapter 6) and then to handle fulfilment in the post-sales phase (chapter 7) of the sales cycle. Without help from a technical representative in the pre-sales phase and without help from the operations team in the post-sales phase, the quality and efficiency of the sales cycle will suffer.

Let's take a typical example of an organisation today where they may have a combination of sales revenue from different business models;

1. Off-the-shelf product (e.g. Televisions) revenue accounts for 30%.
2. Project services (e.g. Televisions, delivery, installation, and configuration) revenue accounts for 30%.
3. Engineering services (e.g. Build the televisions, delivery, install, and configure) revenue accounts for 20%.
4. Distribution channel revenue accounts for 20%.

Naturally, for these four different business models to be successful, they require different sales engagement processes and adequate resource allocation. For that reason, the success factor of a business model depends on a well-defined sales engagement process. In essence, the sales engagement process and responsibilities for each role in the sales cycle can be summed up as follows:

The Salesperson:

- Qualifies potential business opportunities and presents the value proposition intending to close deals at an efficient rate.
- Establishes and develops a healthy sales pipeline for continued growth.

- Ensures customers are happy by resolving complaints and escalations promptly.
- Manages the commercial relationship, retains and develop the customer to fatten their share of wallet (SOW).
- Works in tandem with the Sales Engineer and employees from different levels of the customer's organisation to identify new business opportunities.

The Sales Engineer (or Technical Representative):

- Positions long-lasting engineering projects.
- Puts the value proposition into physical practice.
- Ensures customers are happy by providing technical insights and technical guidance around the deployment and implementation of the purchased solution.
- Works in tandem with the salesperson and employees from different levels of the customer's organisation to identify new engineering business opportunities.

The Operations team:

- The operations team ensure customer satisfaction while providing adequate support in both the pre-sales and post-sales phase. The operations teams can be various departments from product management, project management, order processing, supply chain, finance, and others. They are also responsible for taking care of hard-earned customers through various pre-sales and post-sales activities.

Depending on the solutions complexity, the segment in which you sell your solution and your sales engagement process, the sales cycle duration can vary in length from hours to days, weeks, months, or even years. Through experience, we learn that the average salesperson selling an end-to-end IT/ICT conceptual solution in the B2B sector can close new customer acquisition deals within three to ten months. Appropriate support from within the salesperson's organisation is necessary to keep these deals on track and ensuring post-closing integration success.

Milestone # 4 – Deal Won (Contract Awarded)

Well done! The deal is sealed, and the contract is signed. It's the end of the pre-sales phase and the beginning of the post-sales phase. After all the hard work you've put into making the sale, it's time for the next phase. There are several things to do that will help you retain and develop your relationship with this customer for the long-term.

Once a customer awards you the contract, you and your organisation's operational excellence are committed to delivering on that promise. Again, honesty and trust are essential. If you offer a discount to close the deal which your organisation can't deliver, this can wind up haunting you not just in your relationship with this customer, but in the future, as it affects your reputation as a salesperson and, in turn, your brand and that of your organisation.

During the pre-sales phase (milestones 1, 2 and 3), you and the customer should have already assessed the risks and opportunities that could occur both beneficial or harmful for the successful delivery and implementation of the ordered solutions. However, delivering on the promise is a task for your entire organisation and relies on the health of your organisations operational excellence. While leaders know that winning deals is a team effort, some still struggle to understand what effort lies behind closing deals and the support the salesperson requires during the entire sales cycle. Genuine leaders don't only allocate revenue targets productively among sales teams and regions, but they also ensure each has sufficient resources to execute their tasks smoothly. This resource allocation will impact how the organisation can deliver on its promises and build relationships with customers. It's quite simple: for an efficient sales cycle, salespeople need adequate support not only in the presales phase (milestones 1, 2, and 3) but also in the post-sales phase (milestone 4 and 5) to retain and develop the customer further.

The moment salespeople receive the purchase order from a customer, they need to hand it over to the operations team (e.g. project team or sales support team) to handle the fulfilment of the goods' delivery and complete the installation. This is where a kick-off meeting takes place to handover the order to the operations team. In the fulfilment stage, the salesperson works in close collaboration with the operations' team. Though the salesperson is still the single point of contact towards the customer, much of the post-sales activities (fulfilment stage) are out of their control. Rightly so since the salesperson must now focus on closing more new deals.

While the project management team is a separate department to those of the operations team, the project manager (PJM) can become more active in the post-sales phase. Still, the involvement of the PJM in the pre-sales or post-sales phase depends on an organisations' set-up, business model and processes. As described earlier, depending on where your organisations' business model generates its revenue between off-the-shelf products, project services, engineering services or other revenue income sources, this dictates the amount of work done by the PJM in the pre-sales and post-sales phase. For that reason, the handover process from a salesperson in the pre-sales phase to a PJM in the post-sales phase (fulfilment stage) is a critical undertaking. The pre-sales is where the PJM (or operations team) comes in for the fulfilment of the duties defined in the sale.

The kick-off meeting with the PJM is where the salesperson provides all the details that helps the PJM get a clear understanding of the scope, time and cost for the project. Though the PJM might be involved in the pre-sales phase, the salesperson still needs to provide them with all the details during the handover kick-off meeting. The kick-off meeting could also be a brainstorming session on how to best implement the project. In the context of project management, the brainstorming session is a technique where a group produces ideas that contribute to the successful implementation of the work done in the project. For example, let's say you are brainstorming for a trekking vacation; your brainstorming approach could be:

- Trekking location ideas (Where is the destination going to?)
- Prioritise (Why is this the right journey to take for the destination?)
- Requirements (What is needed for the journey and destination?)
- Plan (Where does the journey begin?)
- Risk (What should I consider paying attention to on my journey?)
- Method (How can I ensure a comfortable journey for reaching the destination?)
- Lessons (What have I learned from other journeys?)
- Results (Was my trekking journey a success?)

Like in sales, project management has strategic work elements, and much of the project managers' effort across the project's lifecycle will be driven by the project owner (customer) or sponsor.

The job of a PJM is usually a temporary project-based role where they are responsible for scheduling the resources needed to complete the project and manage project costs. The PJM can use technology to measure cost, productivity, and progress through the project's full lifecycle. They usually create a project plan which is a tool that helps the PJM manage and control resource usage and monitors the tasks to ensure successful project completion. Since the project may have numerous tasks to complete, the PJM examines activities that can be done simultaneously and those done in chronological sequences. This will result in the PJM having a detailed list of people involved in the project and a list of all the tasks they can prioritise and examine whether their organisation has the technology or expertise to do it themselves. If they don't have the technology or expertise, they would outsource these tasks or even acquire the needed technology to complete the project.

Why Was a Deal Lost?

When the deal is lost, the salesperson performs a structured post-mortem analysis. They will need to understand why they lost the deal by interviewing the customer. Learning the reason for losing also shows the customer that the salesperson's organisation is looking for improvements.

Before archiving the post-mortem results into the CRM system, the salesperson reviews the questionnaire results with their peers and manager to decide what actions (if any) to take next.

To perform a structured post-mortem analysis, you can use a word document to complete the interview questionnaire with the following five sectors and questions, but one still needs to brainstorm on questions that fit your organisation best:

1. Contract reward
    - How many proposals were submitted?
    - Who won the contract?
    - How did your proposal (scope, time and costs) line up with the other proposals (e.g. 2nd, 3rd, or 4th place)?
2. Decision Criteria and Weighting
    - What price won the tender (e.g. 10%, 15%, 20% or lower than yours)?
    - How did the customer overall rate your proposal and understanding of their needs and requirements (e.g. from 1 to 10 - 10 being the best mark)?
    - What qualities (advantages) or strengths (benefits) stood out at the winning firm that were missing in yours (e.g. relationship, trust, the competition understood the customers challenges better, they weren't convinced with your solution, the competition offered more options to select from, etc.)?
    - What threats or weaknesses did the customer identify while interacting with you and your organisation?
    - Who had the influence over the final selection decision?
3. Proposal submission
    - What was the customers' impression of your submitted proposal (what was missing, too much, etc.) and were you compliant with the tender requirements (e.g. regulatory and mandatory elements, content, format, layout, etc.)?
    - What was the customers impression of your organisation (e.g. innovators, trustworthy, competent, etc.)?
    - What advice would the customer give you to help improve?
4. Conclusion:
    - What lessons were learned?
5. Next Steps:
    - What are the next steps (if any)?

Milestone # 5 – Retain and Develop the Customer

In milestone five, your organisations' operational excellence should have grown the customer experience by delivering the components on time and in a flawless condition. Also, the PJM (or operations team) met the installation requirements, and the customer is pleased with the results in selecting your organisation as their new incumbent.

In milestone five, the salesperson now begins to retain and develop the customer further by restarting the entire five milestone process. They now focus on:

- Cross-selling other products and services to fatten the SOW.
- Up-selling to higher-margin products or lower-cost products
- Boost margins by reducing discount levels or increasing the price.
- Protect margins by not giving away free accessories.
- Whenever possible, renegotiate existing price agreements.
- Renegotiate price agreements at the end of the contract term.
- Ensure during product transition you can optimise margin.

The fundamentals of sales are based upon inspiring, persuading, and leading people into taking action. Salespeople should show empathic concern and connect the dots between a customer's business needs and personal needs.

Chapter 8

Build Rapport Before Negotiating

Building rapport in the sales cycle requires more than your personality. It takes discipline to ensure proper preparations are taking place across the entire sales cycle.

- What is Rapport Building? Rapport is the basis for creating a conversation, or relationship based on mutual respect, appreciation and trust. Building rapport means diving into the world of your counterpart to establish a connection and accept everything that is.
- Why is rapport useful? It is the basis of every successful interaction, whether in a counselling situation, a therapy session, an employee interview, a customer meeting, or during an outdoor conversation. Good rapport ensures you can engage and build a relationship with your counterpart at a process level, not necessarily at a subconscious level.
- What can you do with good rapport? You create a trusting basis within a conversation. Your counterpart will quickly feel comfortable and understood. You signal that "we are complementary", but not complicit, thus making others more receptive to change, further development and interaction.
- How does rapport work, and when do I know it's achieved? Building rapport is taking your counterpart on a journey. This voyage means "entering their world".
- What value is in building rapport? Rapport enables your counterpart to reach their destination more efficiently. You will be a better communicator and can quicker transmit your goals to every counterpart.

Building rapport and establishing win-win relationships is a mapping process:

- mapping an adequate solution to the customer's demand.
- mapping the sales approach to the customer's desired pace.
- mapping your product positioning to the buyer's journey.
- mapping your social style to the buyer's social style.

Remember that negotiations are reached over an extended period, they are unpredictable, and no matter how well you prepare, there is still no guarantee for success. Nonetheless, it's critical to go well-prepared to the negation table, and adequately developing a negotiation-preparation plan will be useful in any case (see chapter 6 under milestone 3).

The twenty-first-century salesperson explores the theoretical and practical aspects of negotiation and influence. While many salespeople spend much of their time negotiating and seeking to influence others, they generally devote little time to prepare for negotiations effectively and to learn how the actual exercise of influence functions. They focus on the results they want to achieve and fail to explore the processes and tactics on which they rely. They fail to see how these could be varied or adjusted to attain even better results.

Negotiation is the attempt to change the beliefs, behaviours, and emotions of others. You can achieve better results by using several tactics and considerations such as:

- When you don't consider the three most common pitfalls in negotiating and influencing:
  - When you are not negotiating for yourself, you usually set expectations lower.
  - Not identifying a specific situation as an opportunity to negotiate further.
  - Not being willing to say no.
- Developing relationships before you begin actual negotiation through the reciprocity principle to uncover similarities, areas for genuine compliments and collaboration, or favours to return. The reciprocity principle is the desire to return a favour or gift when something is received. Here, remember to follow your organisations code of conduct guideline to not breach them with the reciprocity principle.
- Gathering statistics on common practice from independent consumer reports can be helpful to secure customer agreement. People tend to follow the lead of those similar to them, so show others' responses, testimonials, case studies, and past successes.
- When a customer becomes rude, it is not an excuse for you to be nasty. Be professional and don't take things personally. For instance, customers understand salespeople have a private life and usually call only during office hours. You will still find more demanding customers, but you should learn to hold them in check and treat each customer accordingly.
- Using of the mirror effect: if you want politeness, be polite to others, and if you want aggression, be aggressive. The mirror effect is how you perceive yourself through the eyes of others around you. Carefully observe comments or body posture of others to see that part that is the reflection of you.

It requires much attention and observation skills to achieve the best outcome.

- Working with the similarity principle in which we tend to feel relaxed with, and more persuaded by, people who are similar to us in belief, appearance, culture and ethnicity, language, sense of humour and profession. Of course, bias should not be countenanced, and many of these factors cannot be changed, but consider the ones you can adopt — such as the social style.
- Being reliable and showing integrity. Does your approach to negotiation follow your organisation's policies, its code of conduct guidelines, your ethics, and your negotiation counterpart's expectations of appropriate behaviour? In turn, when you believe that misconduct has occurred, call it out. Name what they are doing and notify them carefully of your perspective.
- Considering how would awareness and approval of your product, service, organisation, or personal brand be affected if it were exposed to public scrutiny?
- Not making false/fraudulent deals with customers, friends or family to inflate one's KPI's because they might be severe retributions.
- Sales is about teamwork, so you better pick your own negotiation team members carefully. To ensure negotiations are meaningful and move successfully, you might even request that certain individuals attend or do not attend negotiation meetings.
- While people who regularly work together tend to reach an agreement and have goodwill for each other, they may still engage in aggression. For instance, when the sales engagement process is unclear, some tend to handover unreasonable workload for the sake of achieving their KPIs. However, try not to overreact, except theatrically, and only when you learn to be aware of the other person's negotiating tactics will you be able to respond appropriately.
- Practice empathy by getting a direct experience of another person's life and then walking a mile in their shoes. Listening is one of the most important ways you can show empathy, and this means truly listening free of prejudice, discrimination, and emotions.
- Begin negotiations in a way that leaves room to make exceptions, and expect concessions in exchange. Make clear that this is the first offer, and use the prospect's response to determine the range of possible agreements. However, to avoid losing credibility in your pricing structure or if the price is the essential deciding factor for your customer, you should ensure the price in your initial offer can be reduced by up to 15% to close the deal because if the customer rejects your initial offer and you provide an additional 30% discount, you risk losing credibility towards the customer, and this will become your brand.
- Another important factor to consider is the coalition principle. When the

majority of people in a group agree, it becomes challenging to change that coalition's consensus.

Whenever the buyer isn't open for further negotiations, evaluate whether you have assessed their needs properly. Remember both the customer and your organisation have walk-away criteria if either party is not willing to move. Some salespeople and organisations are likely to exit when competitors initiate a fierce bidding war. Naturally, organisations that have a defined negotiation process increase their bottom-line profitability more efficient.

Negotiations in the Sales Cycle

Though negotiations are ongoing activities, negotiations in milestone 3 of the five sales cycle milestone (discussed in chapter 6) can be a daunting and challenging task, and it's a skill in and of itself. The following is a list of some prerequisites before entering negotiations:

1. **Predict a positive vision of your goal**: Try to make a predictive mind map on how you can envision the sequence of the negotiation. Successful salespeople are negotiators with an excellent predictive vision of success. They fully understand the subject matter, and they have a firm grasp of negotiation process requirements. They work towards building a win-win results for each party to achieve their objectives.
2. **Define your strategy**: When you assess your organisation's limits and desires, this also defines your walk-away price. When this assessment is done beforehand, you will be well prepared to negotiate with greater confidence. This approach enables flexibility, and you will notice a point at which you may need to stop the negotiation, persuasion and influencing.
3. **Your Negotiation style**: By understanding the different negotiating styles, you can be better prepared for different situations. Negotiation style refers to the negotiators' personal behaviour used to carry out the negotiation strategy. According to an exploratory study on negotiating styles, the Vikalpa journal published research results pointing to four possible negotiation styles adopted by people: Analytical, Equitable, Amicable and Aggressive. Though other different negotiation styles for dealing with the stressful and high-pressure situation may exist, there is no single best approach since the approach is determined by the given situation.
4. **Your social/behavioural style**: Salespeople know both their negotiation style and the preferred negotiation style of their counterparts, and they use this understanding to tailor their approach to the social style, behaviour, and the needs of others (we will discuss the understanding of Archetypes and Social Styles

more in-depth in chapter 9). The impact of social styles during the negotiation and influencing stage is too often undervalued. Salespeople who understand these social style differences and adapt their approach to harmonise with the other negotiating party can achieve a harmonious relationship. The negotiation approach that fits us best is connected to our dominant social style, which is an inherent characteristic – unlikely to change, though it can shift with age, situations, and experience. You must remain mindful of how your social style impacts your negotiations with people who have other social styles, different roles, and who come from different cultural backgrounds. Though we cannot change our primary social style, we can develop skills to recognise the social styles of others and be aware of how our style accommodates or clashes with others'. This awareness and adaptation can lead to optimal results.

5. **Proposal (compile options)** - Proposals consist of the conditions and the offering. You want to be innovative by offering your customer options, so in some situations, you might choose to have additional options in your first proposal. In other situations, offering an alternate option may confuse the customer and also dilute your organisation's resources. Here the customers would even expect a lower price point every time you offer a proposal because they usually reject the first one. However, the ideal case is to use good judgment when delivering additional options or an alternative proposal, yet keep both your organisation and your customers best interest in mind.
6. **Tradeoffs in Scope or Time to reduce Costs:** Time to complete an activity is often fixed, and quality standards may differ. Often both parties have issues or questions on price, quality, product or service coverage and tend to negotiate on very few variables until, ideally, they meet in the middle. Each negotiators willingness to make tradeoffs at the negotiations depends on expectations of tradeoffs being equally met for a win-win scenario. The customer knows that time, and cost constraints are consistent, whereas scope and quality mean different things to different people, and this impacts both the time and cost constraint factor. Therefore, while each constraint has one side, changing any aspect of the scope impacts time and cost. That said, select product options or services you can negotiate to agree on being tradeoffs that can help you come closer to a compromise.
7. **Demonstrate empathy to create long-term relationships:** The negotiation stage can also be viewed as preparation for negotiating the next business opportunity. Some customers may even be willing to grant you future business if you can accommodate their request during the initial negotiation phase. Be cautious and think long-term when a customer advances a future purchase because you are not engaging in a one-off commercial transaction; you are building a long-term relationship that takes time and patience, yet it's mutually rewarding.

8. **Ask for the purchase order:** Though asking for the purchase order is irrelevant in the negotiation preparation phase, you should know when to ask for it. At a specific point with your insights gathered from earlier interactions with the customer on their decision-making process (discussed in chapter 14 - Sales Engagement Preparation Plan), you can identify a moment to ask for the purchase as you've addressed the right emotional triggers of the decision-makers. Don't be afraid to ask for the order because, from a psychological standpoint, the customer wants to be asked for the order.

When both negotiating parties follow through on their promises, this strengthens the relationship and builds trust further, thus making it easier to negotiate the next time around.

There are many factors, both inside and outside an organisation that are out of the salesperson's control and can influence the negotiations and sale. For instance, the salesperson has no influence over their organisation's operational excellence to ensure goods are delivered on-time without any defects or missing components or cost control over the project managers plan to have adequate resources allocated and tailormade to ensure the client's overall interests and objectives are met, or control over the correct invoicing sent to the customer after the project completion, etc. All these factors can damage the existing business relationship with no fault of the salesperson.

Another challenge in negotiations that cannot be fixed is the inequalities that come about through our dress code choice, our hobbies, or other material possessions that signal differences when negotiating with people of different socioeconomic levels or cultures. This type of tension that exists between empathy and envy between negotiators of different status, wealth, or the diversity of human cultures is even harder to monitor and control. Everyone you meet is valuable and worthy; therefore, you should learn not to exclude others if their culture, opinions or views differ from yours. As long as you can separate these inequalities from the negotiations and find balanced interests for mutual gain, you will be able to negotiate more objectively.

Decades of research by social psychologists indicate that you subconsciously hold a negative stereotype about a specific group so when you meet someone from that group, you will treat them differently and discriminate them further. It occurs even amongst individuals with the best intentions. This is a sad fact to confront, and it points to the failure to speak up, to address microaggressions, and not let people get away with it.

Everyone has to work to overcome their biases. Especially in the business context, we can often link the challenges found in business performance to an atmosphere in which leaders are not held accountable. Issues such as sexual harassment, ostracism, bias, and defamation of character in the workplace cannot always be avoided, but they can be spotted to minimise the risk of happening twice – learn to see it and stop it. Though it may not be wise or practical to confront the harasser in every case directly, yet preventing harassment should to be everyone's responsibility. The following are a few ways bystanders can get involved when they experience inappropriate conduct from others:

- Don't go in alone – seek support from other people around you to interrupt the situation that will reinforce the idea that the harasser's behaviour is unacceptable.
- Disrupt the circumstance - when you witness someone being harassed, attempt to distract the harasser or involve yourself into the interplay between the harasser and the targeted person to calm the situation.
- Challenge the harasser - cautiously select phrases (e.g. Why would you say that? What did you achieve out of doing that? Do you know how problematic that is?) to inform the harasser politely that they need to stop, and their words or actions are inappropriate.
- Set the expectation on when to speak up - when you experience someone making inappropriate comments or being harassed, you could say, "I think you are a better person than that", or in a group setting, you could say, "Did you all hear what was said?"
- Be proactive and know your position to speak up – when your position, gender, race, age, etc. ease you to speak up, do so, especially when you are not a representative of the targeted group.
- Accommodate the targeted person - express your comfort to the individual by letting them know that what had happened to them isn't their fault and affirm to them that they didn't do anything wrong.

A challenge in negotiations can also come about when either negotiating parties have personal financial issues. When you owe someone money, you are always under an obligation to pay them back. Therefore, personal financial health is also an essential factor in negotiations. That is why the calmness of a CEO or a key decision-maker illustrates that their needs are met, and they have made sure that any potential deals won't threaten them, their families or their organisation. They approach the negotiating table from a position of strength and personal stability.

Exhibit Adaptable Consciousness in a Job Interview

Priscilla, Mark, and Alain had been seated for twenty minutes when Megan entered the conference room in a state of excitement.

Megan was genuinely likeable, and it was nearly impossible to get annoyed with her. Even though she was twenty minutes late, the other three forgave her as soon as she apologised. "I'm sorry for my delay, I just left an exciting training session."

Mark quickly interjected, "Megan, we are already twenty minutes late, and we need the final decision on which business developer to hire. We have all interviewed the three candidates; share your thoughts and recommendations for the one you think we should hire?"

Pricilla reminded the others that she saved the spreadsheet of requirements they agreed upon before they began with the interviewing process and handed them each a copy. As they glanced over the spreadsheet, Mark was the first to comment, "From my brief encounter with the three candidates, Sophia seemed intellectually quick on the uptake, handling all the theory and finance topics without difficulty. She also shared growth plan results she expects to achieve in a presentation she prepared for the interview. Based on her preparation and character, I think she will help grow sales revenues and increase customer retention. In contrast, the other two candidates lacked enthusiasm. they seemed aimless, or bluntly wasted my time with heaps of irrelevant information. I'm ready to decide to move forward with Sophia unless there are any reasons not to hire her. What are your thoughts, Megan?"

Megan replied, "By any standard, Sophia is the right candidate! She is a refreshingly eager and confident applicant. I found her conversational style and attentiveness fitting for the business developer role. When I shared my ideas for sales and marketing activities, Sophia provided examples of how these activities worked well with her previous customers. Sophia shared her vision that was in alignment with my business development strategy as sales director. Besides, have you seen her track-record? I'm impressed by how her career path took off, landing prestigious business deals all along the way. I have some friends at these organisations who know Sophia, and they all praised and highly recommended her. I am for Sophia too."

There was a brief moment of silence, and then Alain said, "I'm glad you think Sophia is the ideal candidate. Out of all the candidates I met, she seemed genuine and authentic in how she would support the operation team in developing an engagement process to shorten the sales cycle. Also, she agreed to help put together win-win SLAs for our aftersales team. One more thing that impressed me about Sophia was her listening skills. I can state with confidence that she and I have a mutual understanding of operational excellence. My gut feeling tells me that Sophia is the best candidate, but I'm curious about Priscilla's decision."

Mark looked at Priscilla and asked, "What are your thoughts of Sophia? Didn't you say she had some methodology that could generate leads as well as improve engagement with customers? What do you think?"

Looking at the spreadsheet she had completed with an analysis of all the candidate's strengths and weaknesses, Priscilla responded, "The answer is yes, I think Sophia is our best option. From my research, I discovered that she has a methodology and technological expertise that facilitates predictable growth. Also, it seems she doesn't overlook the importance of interactions and relationships with customers and co-workers. Sophia was very rational and clearly described each element of her business development approach. She explained in detail how her methodology would help us potentially achieve additional growth. She also explained how traditional lead generation marketing strategies were losing effectiveness in today's digital age. She then demonstrated how neuromarketing messages focusing on the customer buying journey would be more effective in reaching our target audience. "Once again, Mark interrupted, "It seems that we all agree, Sophia is the best candidate. I have another meeting scheduled, so I've got to run. You can all stay to discuss the induction training programme, but for me, I have heard everything I needed to hear."

To reduce the tension of Mark's interruption, Alain said, "I understand that you are in a hurry and we might need to postpone this decision until Priscilla can tell us about Sophia's engagement methods and techniques she used."

Mark replied, "No, that isn't the most important criteria for selecting Sophia. You can continue this meeting to discuss the steps moving forward, but I have to leave. Priscilla, let Sophia know that she's hired and have her contact Alain to go through the SLA. Megan, once Sophia's contract and the SLA details are handled, you can introduce her to the rest of our staff to make her feel at home. I will be on a business trip for a couple of days, so tell Sophia I want to meet her when I return."

Mark left the conference room, and during a brief moment of silence, the three collected their thoughts. After they reflected on their interviews with Sophia, Megan then asked, "Am I the only one who noticed this is the first time that we have all been in complete agreement? Somehow, we've all reached the same conclusion in regard to Sophia. I don't know how Sophia was able to adjust to make us feel comfortable and confident in selecting her as the best-suited candidate. Still, it surely worked because I wanted to hire her in the first few minutes of our interview. I'm eager to learn how to sell, like Sophia."

Priscilla nodded and said, "I found my conversation with Sophia both stimulating and thoroughly enjoyable. She displayed a sense of positive curiosity, and I got the impression that she was 100% authentic. She was polite, genuine, and a real pleasure to meet. She is the first applicant I've met who was able to articulate her interests and reasons for applying in a way that convinced us all. Sophia led us each down a different pathway until all of us individually arrived at the same destination; the decision to hire her."

Alain nodded as Priscilla spoke, and when she was done, he added, "I can't stand pushy salespeople, but Sophia never asked me once to hire her. Instead, I felt like one of her customers who was buying, not forced to buy. It may not sound huge, but from my perspective, it is an important difference from the other candidates. She seemed entirely focused on our need and goals, not on what she wanted, and I was relieved when I heard we all came to the same conclusion to hire Sophia."

Megan looked up and said, "True, I too have dealt with many salespeople, and Sophia has the features of a professional business developer who will generate revenue. I want to learn how she was able to connect differently with each of us. I mean, we four make a great team, but we are still very diverse in our interests and beliefs. How was Sophia able to sway us all to agree on a matter of such importance?"

The answer is that Sophia didn't only focus on mapping her conversation to that of the different buyer's styles of Priscilla, Mark, Alain and Megan but she adopted the discipline for identifying the social and behavioural styles of the four decision-makers that we will discuss in Chapter 9 (Archetypes in Perspective). Fearlessly, Sophia shifted her focus on dialogues that matched the different needs and social styles. Her objective was to show the interviewers how she would provide answers to their problems, without over-promising, over-selling, or overemphasising. She put the needs of the "interviewers" first. In other words, Sophia understood it was never about her; it was how she could solve the pressing problems of Megan, Priscilla, Mark, and Alex.

While being adaptable, you don't change your ideas or opinions. Instead, you can change the way you position them. Adaptable people understand the difference between their inner character — who they are — and their external behaviour, the role in which they put themselves. Adaptability doesn't mean changing your personality, but you can change your behaviour, mindset, and mentality to match others. Adaptable people decide to modify their behaviour in a given situation or event. On the contrary, less adaptable people respond out of habit, regardless of whether the response is appropriate or productive. Since the requirements for any robust relationship are respect, trust, and friendship, you should build rapport with others and hold yourself accountable to deliver performance every step of the way. Only you have the power to set the wheel in motion.

Chapter 9

Archetypes in Perspective

Archetypes are ingrained in the human psyche that plays a role in our personalities and influences our social behaviour. The Swiss psychiatrist Carl Jung believed that the human psyche was made up of three layers. According to Jung, (i) the ego represents the conscious mind, (ii) the personal unconscious contains memories that include the suppressed ones (iii) while the collective unconscious is shared among beings.

- The ego: The term EGO is given as the structure of the conscious mind of all that we are aware of which we refer to as our conscious perceptions, our feelings, thoughts and memories.
- The personal unconscious: These are all our psyche traits that our ego does not recognise which are made up of a psychological trauma we experienced or memories we conceal.
- The collective unconscious: This is the knowledge and experience we share as humans. It is the archive of peace, spirituality, birth, passion, love, anger, evil, death, spiritual, religious, and traditional stories and experiences.

These archetypes are the concept behind all our thinking, our religious and our mythological perceptions. Jung believed that each archetype played a role in personality, but found that most people were dominated by one specific archetype. According to Jung, the actual way in which an archetype is brought into concrete existence depends upon several factors, including a person's cultural influence and personal experience. He identified four significant archetypes but also believed that there was no limit to the number that may exist. These archetypes can't be observed directly but can be inferred by looking at literature, art, religion, colours, etc. The four main archetypes described by Jung are:

- The Persona: The persona is the way we present ourselves to the world. The persona archetype is depicting the mask we put on when we interact with others. It's our public image where there can be many masks for different contextual occasions, and the term persona denotes a collection of all these different masks.
- The Shadow: Every archetype possesses a dark shadow side and light

side. The shadow archetype is not an evil side, it's the unknown side, and we usually fear the unknown. It's the part of us we do not accept or even attempt to understand because the shadow appears to us as weak, inferior, flawed or even a disgusted being of ourselves. It doesn't matter how rich, educated, famous or beautiful you are, as long as you fear that people can see your shadow, you will be insecure. Our shadows are the fear-based parts of ourselves we see as a source of humiliation that we try to hide, usually through some kind of perfectionism. The shadow can bring the most transformative experience in life as it helps understand, acknowledge and accept parts of ourselves which we mistakenly reject. It helps us work with issues of competition, self -doubt, etc. It unlocks our creativity side, helps us reclaim power and authority. It guides our journey from exploration to becoming more self-aware.

- The Anima or Animus: Apart from knowing the persona and shadow selves exist, most people are unaware of their male and female selves within them. The anima is the female residing in the collective unconscious mind of men while the animus is the male residing in the collective unconscious mind of women. According to Jung's words, "The anima is a personification of all feminine tendencies in a man's psyche ". Therefore, it's safe to say that the animus is the personification of all masculine tendencies in a woman's psyche. Both anima and animus archetypes draw their energy from the collective unconscious. The anima and the animus archetypes can be influenced by an individual's unconscious mind that they carried as children usually modelled on primary caretakers, their parents, or the surrogate parents that raised them. This imprint of the anima and animus can influence the individual's relationships with the opposite gender later in their lives.
- The Self: The self is the result of a final product of unity from the conscious and the unconscious mind of a person. According to Jung, the self is a process where a person becomes aware. Compared to the ever-changing ego or shadow, the self is constant and unchanging. Other psychoanalytic theorists describe the self as the stage in which an individual transcends group attachment and narcissistic self-absorption.

Archetypes represent essential attributes of our experience that recollect deep emotions as we evolve, such as reason or scepticism. Though many different archetypes exist, Jung defined twelve primary types that symbolise fundamental human motivations: (i) The Innocent, (ii) Everyman, (iii) Hero, (iv) Outlaw, (v) Explorer, (vi) Creator, (vii) Ruler, (viii) Magician, (ix) Lover, (x) Caregiver, (xi) Jester, and (xii) Sage. Each character has its personality traits, its own set of values and meanings; many people have several archetypes at work within them. Gaining insight into the typical behaviours and motivations of one's archetype can play a significant role in the way we interact with others, especially family, friends, and co-workers.

Naturally, a discussion with a friend or family member will sound different from a report or chat with your boss, but understanding the power of communication will help you in all circumstances. In essence, to be good in something you need to dive into the role. For example, our role as a parent differs from our position as a grandparent, an uncle, a sister, a brother, or any other relative.

Understanding Social/Behavioural Styles

People have been fascinated with social/behavioural styles for centuries, and you might have come across the concept on more than one occasion. In ancient Greece, the physician Hippocrates outlined four temperaments: sanguine, phlegmatic, melancholic, and choleric. Hippocrates described the four temperaments as part of the ancient medical concept of humourism, that four bodily fluids affect human personality traits and behaviours. Modern medical science does not define a fixed relationship between internal secretions and personality, although some psychological personality type systems use categories like the Greek temperaments (Wikipedia). Yet, one of the most influential ideas originated in the theoretical work of the famed Swiss psychiatrist and psychoanalyst Carl Gustav Jung (26 July 1875 – 6 June 1961) in his 1921 published book titled *Psychological Types (Psychologische Typen in German).* In his book, he distinguished two general attitudes as introvert and extravert (see following illustration table). Jung categorised the two general attitudes into four essential functions; thinking, feeling, sensing, and intuiting. These basic styles recur commonly in the discoveries scientists and doctors have made over centuries. Also, despite their differences, Jung believed that an introvert usually marries an extrovert or vice versa. Perhaps it's a case of opposites attracting to achieve a balance of completeness.

Carl Jung's Theory of Personality Types				
Sensation (feeling or perception)		Intuition (Understand instinctively)		Two perceiving or non-rational functions
Thinking	Feeling	Thinking	Feeling	Two judging or rational functions
Extravert	Introvert	Extravert	Introvert	The functions are modified by two main attitude types
Extraverted sensation Extraverted intuition	Introverted intuition Introverted sensation	Extraverted thinking Extraverted feeling	Introverted thinking Introverted feeling	Jung proposed that the dominant function, along with the dominant attitude, characterizes consciousness, while its opposite is repressed and characterizes the unconscious.

People differ in fundamental ways, even though the instincts which drive us can be the same. We all have different learning styles, barriers and challenges in how we can best do whatever it is that we want to do. Despite our best efforts, we all judge others over small things or who behave selfishly or hurts our person, yet judging a person does not define who they are, it defines who you are. However, though we should not judge a book by its cover, in the business development context, the saying holds due to the need for the salesperson to have an element of qualification (or disqualification) at the early stages of the sales cycle. Salespeople instinctively make use of these distinctions when they see someone who they have never met before.

Though classifying people has been criticised as labelling and an exclusionary practice, this same practice applies to many other professions. Many professions work with an understanding of social styles for different purposes. For instance, for the psychiatrist to help patients suffering from a psychiatric disorder, they need to understand the different social style. Without this understanding, they won't be able to diagnose and treat their patients. Also, the importance of a physician and surgeon to grasp the understanding of social/behaviour styles is to improve the counselling aspect. Fact is that no one can influence learning unless they can connect with someone in the first place and communicate effectively. As a salesperson and business developer, you do not need to become a psychologist, but with some basic understanding and attention to human behaviour, you can become better tuned into your customer's social styles and needs.

Getting along with others is a vital success factor to your professional career in sales, and it's one soft skill that successful people have in common. Adjusting to different social/behaviour style without realising it is somewhat human nature. To know how people prefer to be treated requires a basic understanding of the social styles which guides how you behave around them. When you pay attention to the needs of others, you are trying to understand their point of views and their beliefs. Though personalities are ingrained and difficult to change, in certain circumstances, they can change. Therefore, understanding your natural style and learning to recognise other people's is a great start.

If you are new in sales, it will take some time for you to master your adaptation to other social/behavioural styles. The style you identify with then dictates how you adjust yourself to build rapport and find common ground, leading to a win-win outcome. This lets you lead others in a direction they want to go, speak to them in a way they find comfortable (making them likely to listen to a salespersons advice), and sell to them the way they want to buy. Listening to and identifying customer needs teaches you to tailor interaction to social styles and buying habits. Interaction with others can be constructive or destructive, and when someone is unwilling or unable to adapt, they will not gain anyone's trust.

Though many different social styles exist and they depend on a situation one finds themselves in, the qualification (or disqualification) method that worked well for me was taking advantage of four social style types. While these four social styles are dominated by one specific social style, they also have fundamental human motivations of the other three social styles. The reference given to these four social styles are; (i) Control-driven, (ii) People-driven, (iii) Data-driven, and (iv) Conform-driven, which I find easier to visualise. While this list is not exhaustive, it will provide you with some thought as you encounter various social styles.

It will take some time for you to determine your best method, and sadly, there is no shortcut to program your mind to do something new or different. However, this investment in time will pay off over the entire course of your career. It takes a dedicated effort and a personal commitment to develop this skill, but once mastered, it can transform the way you build relationships. When it becomes second nature, you can able to potentially read someone's style as soon as they first meet or speak with them, and it no longer requires so much of your emotional and mental energy.

Given a particular situation, any of the four social styles' objectives or objections may change. There are also certain commonalities with the four personality styles. Naturally, all four social styles prefer to work with people who are efficient, receptive, competent, committed, and communicative. On the other hand, with each of the four social styles, negative traits may accompany positive qualities. Any of the four social styles, when taken to an extreme, has a darker side — such as when under pressure or while relieving their inner tensions. For an organisation as a whole, this darker side can feed into a toxic workplace. That may lead to abusive language, doublespeak, secretiveness, withholding of information, broken promises, neglected responsibilities, and much more. Obviously, all four social styles have the potential to contribute to either a healthy workplace or a toxic one.

Salespeople are then often forced to master different approaches and strategies based on similar encounters and experience they have gathered while progressing their career in sales. For example, let's take a look at the professional boxer Floyd Mayweather. To my knowledge, Mayweather had fifty fights and won them all. All fifty boxers he fought against had different boxing styles, techniques and strategies, but that to the experience he gathered over his boxing career, he was able to adapt his boxing skill set over many years (and fights), leading to his track record as a professional boxer with no losses. While we can't promise a career free of losses to you (though surely, your sales career will involve fewer punches than Floyd's), this agility to adapt is something to aspire to, and it will be reflected in your results.

As a salesperson's career path progresses, they continue to improve their understanding of different social/behavioural styles. They learn that when someone with the people-driven personality meets someone with the data-driven personality, productivity may require the people-driven person to talk less, listen more carefully, and focus on the data-driven facts. Through attention, practice, and commitment, you can achieve higher adaptability and recognise when it is necessary to further adjust to another person's social style. Be tactful, reasonable, and understanding as you practice your interactions. This will always make it easier to realise a winning outcome, whether in private or in business relationships.

Another commonality not only for the four personality styles but for all humans is when there are physical signs of stress levels being too high. Whenever tension is too high, it becomes unproductive, and if tension is too low, there is little motivation to take action. Between these two extremes, there is a zone which is the area of productivity. The level of tension that creates this comfort zone is different for everyone. For this reason, one approach salespeople use to break the ice and reduce the level of tension is inviting the customer for a business lunch. In the customers workplace, you will find existing levels of tension. When you take the customer out of their work-environment and bring them into a more comfortable zone, you will reap more benefits. At the same time, you will have the opportunity to learn the customer's social / behavioural styles in a more relaxed setting. People are more likely to do business with people they like and the idea of a business lunch to discuss the potential of a business relationship is a hidden gem. The shared experience over lunch in which both parties come together in a no-pressure environment is a great way to set yourself apart from the competition. Aim to connect with your prospect on a personal level that doesn't cross any boundaries or create awkward moments. For instance, both parties may have a mutual acquaintance or a common hobby, or they prefer the same cuisine. People won't forget how you made them feel, so make the business lunch a memorable one.

The Four Social/Behavioural Styles Approach

Are these social/behavioural styles reliable? Although our perspectives as humans differ, we are all engaged in improving our results. Therefore, it's important to distinguish between reliability and validity. We can agree that our unique understanding of social/behavioural styles differs in perspective. The social/behavioural style distinction of someone's self-impression is based on others impression of a person which is in contrast to behavioural measurement techniques as you ask people to report about themselves. The self-report data is useful in providing feedback about how someone sees themselves, but their perception differs from those of others who see them in action. That said, the significance given to the four social styles are perspectives based on the lessons-learned mapping, yet this view may not be considered accurate to someone else's perspective and lessons learned.

When a customer discovers that you sincerely have their interests in mind, you gain their trust, and the rest of the sales cycle can continue without much obstacles. This is part of the sales cycle that you have the most influence on, plus its rewards make it well worth mastering. As you read the following descriptions of the four different social styles, try to envision encounters you've had with customers who possess each personality type. Regardless of whether they bought from you, consider whether you would have been more successful if you had adapted your style to match theirs. With what you have learned, consider ways you could have expressed yourself to relate to them even better. Also consider the social styles you see in your co-workers, parents, spouse, children, friends, or neighbours to examine how you could adapt to them to build rapport for a healthier and more productive relationship.

The CONTROL-Driven Style

Someone with the control-driven personality is naturally an authoritarian person in control of a situation. They demand the freedom to manage themselves and others, and they use their drive to become winners. The control-driven person likes to get things done and make things happen. They accept challenges and take authority, diving headfirst into solving those challenges. They tend to be strong, willing, precise, goal-orientated, and competitive. They are also known to be stubborn. They realise that successful results can only be achieved by teamwork, but they tend to take control over others, resulting in low tolerance for feelings, attitudes, or shortcomings among co-workers and subordinates. The constant need to come out on top can be annoying and offensive to others.

For the control-driven person, there is only one way — their way. They like moving at a fast pace and tend to become impatient with delays. Other negative traits are their push for success which includes poor listening and the intense need of other people to help the control-driven person accomplish their tasks even at the costs of others.

They focus on their priorities, which may make them appear distant and cold. Sometimes they will lobby for others to bend the rules to serve their needs. They also have trouble having fun. Usually, they have a specific purpose in mind, and they often intertwine business and friendship. They tend to take themselves too seriously, giving bitterness to their humour at times, and they would benefit from the wisdom of relaxation, laughter, and enjoying the brighter side of life.

Control-driven personalities are motivated to achieve a position with decision-making power. They can be excellent problem solvers, and they see themselves as solution orientated leaders who enjoy the challenges they face. Because of this attitude, they are generally viewed as having a high level of confidence, even when that may not be the case.

The PEOPLE-Driven Style

"People-driven," says it all, because people with this style are friendly, and are seen where there is action. They want fun and live to enjoy life. The people-driven person places more priority on relationships than on responsibilities. They have a positive way of influencing others through a cheerful, attractive character, and they focus on attaining approval from others. Their primary personality strength is in the friendly, enthusiastic, and persuasive way they accomplish their goals. They are open with their thoughts and emotions, but sometimes this is only on an artificial level. On the other hand, they will still be happy to share their thoughts on almost any topic. They tend to work promptly and enthusiastically with others and base their decisions on impulse and feeling. They want to be involved anywhere and everywhere.

However, they become bored quickly and easily, resulting in their stereotyping individuals rather than paying more attention to critical thinking. When taken to an extreme, their behaviour may appear artificial, random, unpredictable, and overly emotional. Someone with a people-driven personality who likes to have fun can, as a result, be talkative, forgetful, or disruptive. They enjoy humour and love to chat, and they can be okay with stretching facts and spinning situations to make their storytelling more captivating. They are happy working with others, but their talkative tendencies, at their most extreme, can lead to doublespeak. Their personality does not respond well to authoritative styles displayed by leaders, and they may get defensive or block collaboration. On the other hand, if a leader inspires someone with the people-driven personality, that leader will find a dedicated and committed employee who works hard.

Those with the people-driven personality are mostly optimistic. They praise and support others to create a positive environment because compliments and encouragement make them feel good, even when directed at someone else. They want to be liked by others, and often succeed: people gather around them because they know how to produce fun and make action happen. Their positive mental attitude and natural orientation towards people make them excellent at establishing connections in networking and socialising events. Their creative minds and communication style are great at painting a picture. They make decisions quickly when they become excited by an opportunity because they often see the benefit before you can point it out to them. These leaders base many decisions on instinct and first impressions.

The DATA-Driven Style

Someone with the data-driven personality is analytical, persistent, and a systematic problem solver who is concerned with accuracy and logic than feelings or control. They prefer dealing with tasks rather than people. They want to avoid embarrassment, and therefore, they are more risk-conscious and feel a need for efficiency. They generally keep their criticisms to themselves instead of telling others what they find deficient or wrong. They share information, whether positive or negative, on a need-to-know basis or when requested, and they do so only when they get assurance that there will be no adverse consequence. Often, their actions may be challenging to analyse. They may appear to be detached or fussy because of their fear of being wrong.

The data-driven person naturally focuses on expectations, processes, and intended outcomes. They like organisation and structure, and seeing things in writing make it easier for them to measure the expectations and feedback of others. Their natural leadership style centres on their ability to provide solutions rather than focusing on interpersonal relationships. They plan and select their relationships cautiously, and therefore, building trust with them often takes time. They don't typically like discussing their thoughts or feelings, and so their non-verbal responses speak volumes. You'll want to watch their body language for indications of how they feel in a given situation. Their habit of thorough preparation helps them minimise the possibility of mistakes, yet for this reason, they dislike last-minute changes and inadequate reviews. They can become perfectionistic and worrisome, both with themselves and with others. Their thoroughness may even lead to the overuse of scarce resources within their organisation. All the same, they are naturally the most creative leaders of the four styles.

They prefer co-workers who likewise promote objectivity and thoroughness in their workplace. To perform well, they must take the time to understand the needs as well as the processes. In comparison to the other styles, they tend to be more concerned about a choice or situation's impact on the big picture of the organisation. They prefer minimum interactions and would rather have short conference calls and meetings.

The CONFORM-Driven Style

The conform-driven person is the most group-oriented of all the four personalities. These individuals are warm, supportive, and predictable leaders. They are natural listeners, and they like to focus on getting acquainted and developing trust to maintain a peaceful environment. The conform-driven person may prefer to stay in an unpleasant environment instead of taking a chance on change for the better. This reflects their natural need for tranquillity and stability. They have a problem expressing their true feelings and speaking up, especially if it creates a conflict. Their need for harmony makes them slower in making decisions, and like the data-driven, they seek to minimise risks in unknown situations, especially when including others in a decision. Someone with the conform-driven personality doesn't like the spotlight. They share credit willingly, they find it hard to say no, and they often allow the more assertive personality types to take advantage of them. They don't easily give up, though, and they believe their actions speak for themselves.

The conform-driven person is a mainstream follower. They display a plain, straightforward, and uncomplicated sense of humour. The best world for their personality is one where everyone is friendly, pleasant, and cooperative. When conflict and stressful situations arise, their tolerance declines, resulting in low performance. On the other hand, they are the best predictors of the four styles. Their greatest strength is in reading others; in fact, one reason they seldom push to get what they want is that they usually don't need to. Since they strive for a relationship based on trust, they become worried if the other party doesn't like what they see or get. When dealing with the conform-driven person, one needs to listen and be sensitive, even more so than with other personality styles.

Chapter 10

Discover Power

A Buddhist quote goes, "Your purpose in life is to find your purpose and give your whole heart and soul to it."

Throughout our lives, we search for this purpose. We get a philosophy degree, learn a trade about the different aspects of how a CNC (computer numerical control) machine works, how an organisation operates, how a political system functions, yet a fundamental subject matter gets left behind: the aspect of learning something about ourselves. That is why many people have discovered the subconscious mind practice through meditation, and they develop it to learn more about themselves. The primary method is the exploration and discovery of oneself through mental training and the development of one's behaviour. When you come into a relationship with your subconscious mind through daily meditation, you teach your conscious mind about the existence of the subconscious functions.

Why meditate if we have an idea about what kind of person we are (and are not) and that state is unlikely to change in ten years from now?

Our preferences and values will be very different ten years from now; we will need to acknowledge and make peace with constant changing beliefs. When our beliefs change while our self-image remains the same, this leads to the conflict to who we are and who we think we are. Changes that happen frequently and unnoticed can be when we are exposed to something we like (or don't like) or the more we want something we cannot get, the more we unlike it. We are aware of what we think about ourself today, but what we believe differs from who we are and what we do. There is a separation of what we want and what we do. What we do is governed not by what we want, but by what kind of person we think we are.

Our life events are the result of the workings of our conscious and subconscious minds using practical techniques through which one can change their destiny, principally by focusing and redirecting this miraculous energy. Making regular, powerful, and positive affirmations will remind your conscious mind of the infinite possibilities and advantages of working with your subconscious mind. Let your subconscious mind conceive that you are working diligently to establish a functioning relationship with it.

There are tremendous power and healing force in your subconscious mind that can heal a broken heart, a troubled mind, or a crippled state. It opens the locked door of the mind and releases you from all physical and materialistic bondages. To reach new heights within your consciousness and discover your subconscious mind's power to understand yourself better, you should embrace your subconscious mind and appreciate it as parts of your collective being. By getting to know this part of yourself, you welcome it back as your inner self. In return, it will engage in a whole new level of collaboration as it reveals itself to you. To accept your inner-self, you first need to know of its existence, which is in itself a challenging task that takes significant amounts of effort to harness the power of the infinite possibilities as it leaves us drained.

Self-reflect for an Enhanced Future

Researchers found youth meditating for the first time accomplished higher indicative emotional intelligence skills, increased restful awareness, improved academic performance, greater capacity for self-control, resilience, and self-reflection. Mindful self-reflection is the first step to meditate.

Meditation can be a powerful tool, but since we have physical and materialistic bondages, and all get caught up in our professional and educational environment, this leaves us with no time for self-reflection which is an integral part of the learning process. Meditation gives you the time to ask yourself questions that challenge your assumptions, thus enabling you to identify any changes or improvements you can make.

Self-reflection is a cyclical process that we can learn through experiences and mistakes, but research shows that we won't make self-reflective changes unless we question ourselves on what our experiences mean and think actively about them. According to researchers, learning traits about yourself results in achieving a clearer sense of purpose, self-acceptance, greater well-being, and happiness. Hence, we become a better parent, spouse, friend, leader, and co-worker.

Ask yourself: How effectively am I performing, and how can I improve on these areas? What are my strengths, areas for improvement, and how well am I progressing?

When you develop a self-reflecting habit:

- It provides you with the ability to become even more effective with your actions.
- It allows you to assess how others react to your interaction.
- You move from experiencing towards understanding these behaviour patterns also observed by others.
- It gives you a structured method for considering what is positive and negative about your interactions with others.

- It shows you areas for improvement and places where you have strengths.
- It enables you to identify what approaches work and which ones don't.
- It creates self-awareness and consciousness in how you make use of an idea.

We purposefully self-reflect on something both consciously and subconsciously, but it isn't easy to self-reflect while activities are happening since there will be other activities going on that requires your immediate attention. When we think about our interactions, what we see is not an actual reality reflection but an altered one. Some people may self-reflect with "I'm an accomplished leader", and others may think "I'm not good enough". Nonetheless, you will become accustomed to challenging your assumptions once you create awareness and implement change. Yet, this is only possible when you are open-minded and ready to think about how to make changes and improvements in your practices. Recording yourself can become a resource where you gain a more in-depth insight into this understanding, which will lead to a natural process of evaluation because we must first see ourselves as to how we appear to others.

The self-reflection and self-awareness stage is also a crucial part of procrastination. Procrastination is a common human experience involving the action of delaying or postponing activities. Though procrastination is often confused with laziness, they are different. It's overcoming the habit of postponing critical activities. When we procrastinate, we are indirectly aware of avoiding the activity in question and that doing so is probably a bad idea, yet we still do it.

We should acknowledge at its core; procrastination is about emotions, not productivity. In a 2013 study, Dr Pychyl and Dr Sirois found that procrastination can be understood as "the primacy of short-term mood repair … over the longer-term pursuit of intended actions." Put simply; procrastination is about being more focused on "the immediate urgency of managing negative moods" than getting on with the task, Dr Sirois said. In this study, they argued that procrastination might be best understood as a form of self-regulation failure that involves the primacy of short-term mood repair and emotion regulation over the longer-term pursuit of intended actions. They also proposed that a temporal understanding of self and the intra-personal temporal processes involved in goal pursuit are necessary to gain a complete understanding of the nature and consequences of procrastination. If procrastination is prioritising the present self-mood over the consequences of the future self, then the increase or decrease in different mood-states can prevent or promote future procrastination.

We all want to be productive, but procrastination and laziness sometimes get the best of us. You can learn as much as you want about self-reflection, self-awareness, self-discipline, motivation, planning or time management, but unless you can make use of what you learn in your daily rituals, thoughts and thought process, it will be irrelevant information your memory stores that won't help you combat procrastination.

There are several proven ways to combat procrastination, and the solution doesn't only involve installing a time management software tool or learning new self-control strategies. It's about managing our emotions differently, working within our resistance level and pushing ourself to get started on the task. It would help if you explored how you prioritise activities based on their potential for mood-regulation instead of the task's importance.

To overcome your procrastination, you first need to accept that you procrastinate. Set your goals and identify how procrastination will prevent you from achieving them. As you begin to create an action plan based on the obstacles you want to overcome, implement this plan and calibrate it as you go along. It's crucial not only to understand the exact nature of a problem you're dealing with or to set clear goals since you are more likely to procrastinate when it comes to vague goals without specific steps (e.g. break down large tasks into small ones) for achieving them. But it's also about setting goals that are meaningful and achievable.

Positive Mental Attitude Predictions

From a salesperson's perspective, a positive mental attitude is one of the most important principles you will need to learn. When salespeople experience rejection, defeat, and disappointment as part of their daily business, thinking negatively won't change a thing.

Salespeople know that whenever there is a failure (negative), an equal opportunity (positive) exists. Let's take a look at the good (positive) and evil (negative) in the Yin and Yang elements. When we speak of moral concepts of 'good' and 'evil' in the Yin and Yang elements, this only arises when we decide to add value to either Yin or Yang to demote the other. The Yin & Yang symbol is an idea that one should not get attached to either Yin or Yang. Since everything in existence has Yin and Yang aspects, they need each other where we should embrace them both. The symbol teaches us the balance in our life can only exist when we allow both the Yin & Yang to coexist as a natural bridge between them.

We all want to come to terms with our flaws and blockages so that we can accept them, grow ourselves and overcome them. The subconscious mind contains our unused potential and personal blockages that can bring us to a halt, making us ineffective in various problem areas of our lives. When you are trapped by your personal blockages, this comes about when you have some hidden fear lurking in your unconscious mind and creating a cloak of safety.

We can refer to the subconscious mind as our light and dark shadows. Being unconscious to our light and dark shadows results in us not seeing what causes the shadows, but we see their effects. Everyone has both a light and dark shadow that needs to be revealed so that the energy captured there can be released elsewhere. The processing of both light and dark shadows is always a positive and negative life event. It means we are in touch with the hidden parts of ourselves. When we awaken these potential transformations within ourselves, almost anything becomes achievable.

The light shadows are our potential and the unexplored fruition existing in our lives. These are the undeveloped gifts, talents, unexplored abilities, hidden desires, and everything possible that is good or excellent. Consider your natural talents, your creativity, your joys, and the trust that thrills you to follow it wherever it leads. On the contrary, the dark shadows are those dysfunctional beliefs, repressed emotions, inner wounds, and grief that usually hold us back. They consume endless amounts of energy, leaving us emotionally drained, concerned, angry, and in a state of despair over what we have set in motion.

To achieve high levels of a positive mental attitude prediction one should emphasis more on working with the shadow (or subconscious mind) archetype. By shining light into your shadow, you can control your behaviour. Still, it takes the willingness to experience the transformation of possible guilt and face past failures that resulted in your shadow at work. To work with your shadow is primarily to support you towards your vision of holistic health and healing. However, there is no physiological map which will correctly align your unique psychological make-up. Getting to know your shadow archetype, engage in an inner dialogue with it, watching your emotional reactions and challenging the good part are all an individual's journey.

Carl Jung eloquently explained the shadow using the metaphor of darkness in one of his many quotes, "Knowing your darkness is the best method for dealing with the darknesses of other people." Jung recognised universal patterns in all stories and mythologies, regardless of cultural heritage, suggesting each human mind contained a shared, universal, primal memory with all others. Distinguishing archetypes in literature outline patterns in the way we similarly all unconsciously respond to at a conscious level. Analysing archetypes brings our unconscious reactions into our conscious mind.

Though we all have our comfort zone and ways of doing things, learning should continue throughout our lives if we are to be well-accomplished rounded human beings. The beauty of learning new material is that you don't need to know everything, just see where this puzzle piece belongs in the big picture. Indeed, you never can learn everything on a particular subject, but as you build a knowledge base, you will discover a few core principles to work from, thus making progress more manageable. That progress could be made towards starting a degree or a different job, getting a promotion, or even creating something new in the world, like your own business. These objectives are all enormous investments that can take a year or more of your life. People invest endless weekends (and weekdays) to accomplish them while others do not feel up to that commitment. Still, a few other elements may hold people back:

- When you are good with the status quo, and see no need to question it, either because of your contentment or out of fear of moving into an unknown space.
- When your anxiety rises when you think of taking on a new challenge and learn the skill on the job.

- When you may already be in way over your head, or you may be at the peak of your success. In some cases, it only feels you're at this level because you are plagued with imposter syndrome, but the hesitation is real either way.
- When your confidence is low as you experience rejection after rejection. You might have been rejected because you were not the right fit for a specific job, or maybe the hiring manager did not realise your real value, but you worry that others will never recognise and appreciate your real worth.
- When you are intimidated because you don't think you have the right credentials, degrees, or competencies that give you the qualification to be considered an expert.

Everyone experiences these feelings sometimes, and many have learned some critical concepts that change the way they react or make decisions. Once you have learned to understand your fears and change your perspective, you can accomplish anything. Let fear wake you up rather than shut you down — have no fear.

Many people have accepted the new paradigm in becoming acquainted with their shadow and have gone through the same process to change the understanding of their inner self. We must identify and heal the wound of "I'm not good enough" on any occasion it arises. When you find yourself with negative loops of thought repeating in your mind, which you sometimes will, you can neutralise the loop by identifying it as belonging to the collective unconscious which is shared among beings, thus nullifying its effect by making it non-personal. The dark shadow must be confronted and addressed to take control of all kinds of problems in our lives because what is not owned by the inner self will reveal itself in the outer world.

Apart from these thoughts and feelings, another challenge lurking in the distance is our growing taste for technology. Fact is, we humans need to altercate and elaborate on the risk social media, apps, and other cutting-edge technologies bring. Though our approach is generally wrong when we consider the internet and other advanced technologies negatively impact our mental health, instead, we might need to accept the fact that we are dependent on the internet and other cutting-edge technologies, and unhappiness can be the trigger of this dependency. We should all to take responsibility for identifying the unhappiness that triggers this dependency. You will not be dependent when nothing is missing in your life but can we, as a society, take on the responsibility instead of pushing that responsibility back to others. If we cannot learn for ourselves and change our behaviour in taking responsibility, we will not be happier in the future. Hence, cutting-edge technology will continue to be part of our lives, and we should view them as practical tools for this era.

Chapter 11

Source of Power in B2B Sales

Leaders and employees strive for smart engagement that leads to enthusiasm, motivation, and productivity, not burnout. In order to develop an optimal level of engagement and commitment, it's crucial to provide employees with success factors. These are tools and resources they require to do their job well, to feel worthy of their work, and to recover from the stress they experience through work.

Real leadership, is about developing people, being transparent, displaying integrity, and equity, not self-gratification, allowing everyone to have a voice and a time to share. When leaders create inclusion, employees feel valued, and this appreciation transforms into increased productivity. The flow of communication and trust then spreads throughout the entire organisation as there is a mutually respectful atmosphere. Departments create mutual relationships for a smooth engagement process during the whole sales cycle, making the organisation productive and sales-ready.

Each department of an organisation can be defined, if you will, as a subunit in itself, with different priorities, a different set of KPIs, norms, values, and beliefs. This is also true of each individual within the organisation. The most valuable employees want to be allowed to participate in problem-solving and be involved in decisions-making process on issues that concern how they can effectively do their job and achieve the organisation's goals. Therefore, each subunit wants to take charge of a situation; it works with its own culture and focuses on attaining its own goals. When a weak subunit limits the organisation's performance, strengthening another subunit won't make the intertwined system stronger. Sometimes conflicting or split objectives come about because different departments in an organisation have different sets of priorities. For example, an efficient credit and collections process is as valuable for the sales department as it is for the finance department since both departments want customers to settle payments on time. However, a workforce with a strong sense of customer experience is worth far more to the sales department than it is to the finance department which, unfortunately, is sometimes reflected in how the finance department allots resource budgets. Another challenge is that many organisations use the same pre-sales resources to close deals for national and regional sales teams.

Obviously, this creates a conflict of interest between national and regional business opportunities since they constantly compete for those scarce resources.

The fact is that leaders today are trying so hard to keep up with technological enhancement and sustainability that it's hard for them to slow down and make fundamental changes to the way they acquire, maintain, and develop their employees. Many HR (Human Resources) teams may have diversity programs in place that focus more on creating a diverse workforce than on the harder job of fostering inclusion. When businesses fail to make those outside the dominant zone feel welcome proactively, they lose the insight that people with different backgrounds or experience can bring to the table. Additionally, when employees don't have basic guidelines around what is standard or relevant behaviour – in the form of a code of conduct and documented best practices – the result is often confusion, redundancy, and impaired or even abnormal functioning. Along with providing these, leaders should re-evaluate their engagement processes during the entire sales cycle by asking employees how and where they can improve productivity, enhance performance, and increase engagement, thus improving customer retention.

Employees (and people in general) instincts make them aware of something being authentic or not. In the workplace, they know when they are mistreated or excluded from critical decisions. Workplace ostracism leads to unproductive and unpredictable behaviour. It's one of the causes of disengagement in the workforce and costs US organisations between $450 (€ 379 billion) and $550 billion (€ 463 billion) each year in diminished productivity.

In this context, some leaders make grave errors by remaining narrow in their views, failing to question their assumptions or seek input from their employees. If leaders are unwilling to listen to suggestions or consider others' opinions, they are not serious about establishing consciousness. A leader who is unable or unwilling to relate to an employee's situation or work towards addressing their concerns will have difficulties retaining employees.

Corporate Culture on the Top Shelf

Today, we see trainers, coaches, consultants and other services partners doing an excellent job for an organisation's sales department performance by clearing immediate sales roadblocks with products and services that deliver better strategy growth planning and optimisation in business development. However, sales performance assessments or training for salespeople is not a guarantee for improving an organisation's overall performance; they are part of a series of actions. There is no doubt that consultants and organisations that offer sales department performance services make sense in many instances, but is sales performance really the organisation's biggest challenge, or is a corporate culture challenge impacting the organisation's growth performance? Salespeople rarely fail because of experience, intellect, or skills, but many fail due to the organisation's conflicting business KPI's or an unhealthy corporate culture. Therefore, where business development is a challenge, it is usually because the organisation's corporate culture challenge impacts the execution of their business strategy.

Many leaders have accepted that a productive corporate culture profoundly improves growth. They understand that ensuring employee' goals are realistic, balanced, and supported with the appropriate resources will contribute to their achievements in a sustainable way. They persistently work to understand their corporate culture's challenges, own them, and calibrate it to address them. An organisations corporate culture is the best business growth engine. Plus, an insightful reframing of your workplace situation brings out new patterns to identify advantages or weaknesses.

Trends and challenges are forcing organisations to re-evaluate their business strategy to ensure that not only their corporate culture but their business model and sales strategy are still attractive for their intended purpose. Therefore, once you develop the ability to detect elements of a toxic workplace, you will dramatically improve your effectiveness in judging, influencing, and growing a productive workplace.

Some organisations today don't have a corporate culture design; they instead have multiple goals and initiatives that symbolise progress but fail to come together. These organisations lack any approach to accomplishing that progress other than investing more and trying harder. Corporate culture reveals the truth about employee job satisfaction, employee motivation, and performance. If employees aren't happy, the organisation probably won't be successful.

Corporate culture means different things to different people. The working definition can be described as; the long-standing, implicitly shared values, beliefs, and assumptions that influence people's behaviour, attitudes, and meaning within an organisation. Most can agree that corporate culture is a set of practices, behavioural principles, and beliefs that form an organisation's true identity. Several studies exist going back to the 1980s, explaining the connections between corporate culture and organisational productivity, including the role corporate culture plays in creating a competitive advantage. They presented hard evidence on organisations' cultural and behavioural aspects intimately linked to both short-term performance and long-term survival in terms of return on investment and other financial indicators. The findings are that organisations with a participative culture reap an ROI nearly twice as high as firms with less efficient or engaged cultures.

The fundamental ingredient in a corporate culture's design is a conclusion about the thoughts and behaviour of others. For examples, during a merger, it's difficult for a merged organisation to take on the culture of the merging organisation quickly because employees seldom replace their values and beliefs all at once. Generally, when mergers occur, they bring shifts in leadership principles, practices, and strategies that will have a range of implications for the people in the organisation. A sudden shift in these practices brings disruption and unease. It's a big mistake to assume that employee issues are easy to overcome. Proactive and long-term intervention is necessary to resolve them, and CEOs who fail to recognise when these are happening, end up regretting it.

A productive corporate culture (or workplace) has many correlations in its design. It coordinates principles, policies, and resources while putting them in action to accomplish the organisation's goals. A clear sense of priorities and disciplined focus is required since the more dynamic a challenging situation is, the poorer the foresight. In these situations, agility is essential. Like in a game of chess, a piece is moved into a position that increases its playing options, while at the same time decreasing the options of the opponent's pieces. It's quite similar in the context of business and strategic work; pick objectives that put you in a position to increase your options (e.g. focus on quick wins, low-hanging fruits, etc.), especially relative to your targeted customer's demand.

Corporate culture is an interconnected construction, a living entity, influenced by coordinated actions. The moment you optimise any one part of an organisation without optimising the others, that optimisation may pose challenges for those other subunits. Most of the work in corporate culture design is figuring out these interactions and trade-offs. Regardless of your organisation type, consider these questions: what single, feasible objective, when accomplished, would make the most significant difference in overall business performance? How does this objective impact targets and indicators in other parts of the organisation?

In any event, an unproductive workplace does not arise simply from the absence of a code of conduct, though lack of one can be a warning sign. Instead, it grows out of specific misconceptions and leadership dysfunction due to some leaders lacking the motivation to understand and deal with these tricky fundamentals and how to master them. An unproductive workplace comes about from miscalculation. Mistakes and errors can occur when assessing the challenges presented by the constant disruption of innovation and technology, or when assessing one's resources, new hires, and lessons learned. A miscalculation, however, is not the only source of an unproductive workplace; one can also come about when leadership actively avoids the hard work of crafting a productive workplace. Too often, when leaders are unwilling or unable to understand a situation, they prefer not to make any decision at all.

Even when corporate culture objectives are set, they are unsuccessful when they fail to address critical issues or when they are impracticable. Despite an organisation's best efforts to create productive corporate cultures, too often, leaders can end up creating an unproductive workplace for their employees leading to over 50% of missed or lost revenue where these employees have no resort or are afraid to speak up. Your corporate culture is more than just hiring the right people and retaining them in a healthy work environment. It's also about learning their character, which determines how they act on a day-to-day basis. For that reason, a leader's behaviour matters, for better or worse.

To control your corporate culture productivity, organisations should delegate responsibilities appropriately and add emphasis on creating a unified, transparent, and engaging communication experience. Such collaborative undertaking typically combines centralised (leaders) and decentralised (employees) leadership activities done annually or, where an initiative is a multiyear grant, biannually. This approach is usually undertaken for two reasons: (1) digitisation initiatives are planned to coexist with the organisation's fiscal year targets, and (2) ongoing initiatives are determined by the funding an organisation grants for that specific initiatives priority. The right combination is when senior leadership members and general staff from different parts of the organisation who have critical insight and have conducted their due diligence where the senior leadership evaluates and acts on these results. These are the employees present and run the business, and they understand how it works in practice. They have better oversight and understanding of what other employees will or will not respond to than any leader ever could, especially during mergers. Although some large organisations may assign corporate culture responsibilities to a Chief Culture Officer (CCO), a full-time position is unnecessary for most businesses, nor should your first choice be your HR team. Everyone cannot do everything in an organisation; therefore, breaking up the responsibilities is essential, and remember that it's not only the salesperson's responsibility to ensure the best customer experience, but it's in every employee's interest to achieve a productive workplace, especially the CEO.

Use Leverage for Sales Growth

We realise through experience and research that a more significant challenge comes from the product TTM period. It's no secret that most new products miss their target launch date. Therefore an organisation's product development team has an enormous potential to reduce the new product TTM period because this automatically shortens the sales cycle and enables salespeople to close more deals within a given financial year. When an organisation lacks an action plan to speed up TTM, this creates a bottleneck of potential transactions in the sales pipeline that salespeople cannot close, resulting in lower KPI achievements in that financial year. Another product TTM challenge is when start-up entrepreneurs build a new product from scratch where during the product development phase, they bring together the best minds in the industry to create a new product. Still, in this process, some tend to forget the importance of involving the people who repair the product and the salesperson who will finally position it. They fail to recognise that one can build the best or fastest formula one car, but without a good pit crew and driver, your probability of winning a race is relatively low.

Innovation and product TTM can be a frightening idea for those who don't work in this space as it changes the way work gets done and confronts the uncertainty of how to deliver value. Achieving the right balance and results depends on several internal and external factors and a carefully managed process. Innovation in both product development and business optimisation can be divided into different phases. Each phase has several milestones and only after each milestone is complete will the next step begin. Though this step-by-step approach leads to better control of time, money, resources, quality, and successful results, one should focus on the critical path of the goal where tasks or activities can be sequential as well as parallel.

To consider the context of innovation in your business optimisation initiative, think about aspects like:

- How is the innovation for business optimisation initiatives being led in your organisation today?
- What are the set boundaries (what are your business optimisation initiatives attempting to solve, what types of response are you seeking, and which seem satisfactory)?
- Who is involved in enhancing innovation to optimise business performance?
- What (if any) are the overall organisational implications of the optimisation initiative?
- What is the health of your workplace, and how will the optimisation initiative impact business performance for better or worse?

The internal and external factors for innovation in product development are similar to those involved in business optimisation initiatives, with a few additional aspects, such as:

- Lessons learned from successful and unsuccessful experiences.
- Direct customer feedback.
- Insights and trends are suggesting where your market segment is heading.
- What the "www" (world wide web) says about your organisation - how are your products reviewed and recommended on e-commerce websites, blogs, or social media?
- Competitor analysis.
- Which of the three goal-driven approaches the organisation gives its product teams when developing a new product:

    1. Problem -> they provide the product management team information about the problem at hand and tell them to find a solution to solve this problem.
    2. Solution -> they tell the product management team, "This is the solution we want. Build it."
    3. Metric -> they provide the product team with metrics to achieve

within a given timeline, such as product features, functions, development costs, or proper dimensions (e.g., weight, height, and length) and leave them to develop a product that fits these metrics.

People don't really like change, and innovation can signal discomfort and uncertainty to many. This is when your corporate culture should kick in to welcome transformation since some of the TTM challenges come from issues related to the organisation's corporate culture.

A productive corporate culture is a critical ingredient for an organisation's success, particularly in the area of sales performance and revenue growth. Besides, a productive corporate culture with a well-designed business development strategy produces cost-effective benefits for other parts of the organisation. The measurement of something as complex as an organisation's corporate culture has been a matter of much debate. Some argue that this culture should be intuitively sensed rather than measured, while others say the best way to uncover it is learning from business ethnographic studies and analysis of the stories and situational accounts that make up the folklore of every organisation. CEOs and leaders do not usually have the time to reinvent the organisation's corporate culture or business strategy; they instead complement their existing strategies with lessons learned.

The lesson to be learned about a productive corporate culture is that it shortens product TTM and creates an efficient sales cycle. Its counterpart, the toxic corporate culture, elongates these factors, creating costly, lengthy product TTM and inefficient sales activities, plus the workplace suffers from high employee turnover rate. A productive corporate culture is a vital success factor for overall sales performance, which is, in turn, a critical factor for the bottom-line success or failure of an organisation. The economic investment to achieve a productive corporate culture is more than justified by the better engagement and collaboration that result. When a cultural strategy is well-designed and executed from all parts of the organisation, it's far more likely to result in a positive return on investment. Product innovation leads to a shorter product TTM and increased revenue growth results from a shorter sales cycle. These benefits are so widely recognised that it has become increasingly common for larger organisations to institute a new role, the CCO: Chief Culture Officer. A full-time position is not necessary for most businesses, but an understanding of the dynamics involved will make any employee an asset to the health of their workplace, both socially and financially.

Consider External Forces

Besides constructing a productive corporate culture, establishing a connection to your audience and mapping your offering with their every need, it's also helpful to consider the external forces affecting business performance.

Organisations have to keep their competition in check, which is also an essential part of the business development process. The competitor analysis is a good approach to assess how you level with your competitors. For that reason, organisations pay attention to today's immediate competitors and recognise other sources and types of direct and less direct competitors to which the organisation should attend too.

In today's business climate, competition is higher than ever. This is especially true because technology enables customers to learn far more on their own before reaching out to an organisation to purchase their products and services. Some have bypassed the need to interact with a sales professional entirely by researching and ordering products online. The internet has produced businesses' opportunities to preserve profit margins from traditional growth strategies by using the resources it offers for product innovation, branding, and marketing communications while keeping expenses low. However, these factors don't counterbalance the modern forces making the competition they face steeper, namely:

- The number of businesses providing goods and services enables any organisation to reproduce another organisation's product or service, turning even new high-end product offerings and new technologies on the market into commodities.
- The internet has reduced entry point barriers, meaning that organisations have more new competitors from across the globe. An example of internet opportunities or benefits can be seen when an organisation decides to drive more traffic on social media platforms with triggered marketing and advertising promotions as the target market segment is most active. Globalisation has caused the supply of products to grow relative to the demand for them, further intensifying competition. The internet and mobile technology have also created greater price transparency. Customers can more easily compare prices than ever before.
- Customers have control over when and how they are exposed to an organisation's message, through advertising or other means. They are more likely to create their impressions based on sources a company cannot control, such as reviews, complaints on social media or word of mouth.
- A group purchasing organisation (GPO) leverages the purchasing power of a group of businesses to acquire discounts from vendors based on the collective purchasing power of the GPO members. There are many benefits to joining a purchasing group, such as lower cost of goods purchased from vendors, lower shipping costs, centralised ordering, and support from the GPO itself. However, due to the purchasing power from a GPO, this situation negatively impacts the salesperson's organisations margins as they are now forced to give higher discounts to close the deal with the GPO.

PART III - Develop an Action Plan

"As we grow older and wiser, we begin to realise the only thing that matters is you had brought values of integrity, courage, honour and purpose in life."

Chapter 12

Strategic Organisational Capabilities

In a salesperson's career, many will experience the complex challenges sales departments face and learn the possible responses to these challenges. How they handle these is important due to the sales department being one of the most critical departments in an organisation because if you don't sell someone else will.

One lesson they learn is that an assessment of the organisation and its customers is a vital first step when a salesperson begins a new job. This assessment helps the salesperson understand the following:

- What is the overall health of the organisation and its operational excellence? What challenges exist within it, what mitigations are in place to solve them and how does the organisation work to create the best customer experience?
- Who are the top customers? How much revenue did they generate over the past three years? What products sell better than others, and which products bring in the highest margins? Which regions are performing better than others, and why?
- What are the short, mid and long-term goals of both the organisation and its customers? Also, what action plan does each organisation have in place to achieve these goals?

To design a business development strategy, the salesperson has to assess their organisations' capabilities. Lessons learned from an organisation's past endeavours will ease appraisals of its future possibilities. This assessment helps with creating the business development strategy where the salesperson diagnoses the current situation as they begin to gather historical data that enables them to understand the obstacles they need to overcome and make predictions of a vision to where they want to be (goal or objective). To achieve this vision, they will require an action plan to overcome the obstacles discovered while gathering historical and present data. Yet, no matter how well you plan trajectories in life, something unexpected will always happen. Learn to be agile and adapt to unforeseen circumstances that can easily disturb your action plan.

The stakes for a salesperson are continuously high, and the competition is always close, so when you make a plan, try to stick with it. However, when salespeople recommendations on business development strategies are denied or rejected because of the failure to relate to the salesperson's perspective who understand their assigned customer better and can predict demand and preferences, the salesperson will struggle. Yet, they will still make the best out of any given situation, but they may fail to work towards achieving or over-achieving their annual sales target.

That said, when salespeople start a new role, they usually begin learning and using the organisation's CRM or ERP tool to extract customer information on which to base their assessment and possibly develop a SWOT analysis. The extracted customer data will also provide an overview of what should potentially be their next year's sales revenue targets predictions.

An assessment in the form of a SWOT (strengths, weaknesses, opportunities, and threats) analysis may be conducted when the salesperson is first hired (with an outside-in view of the organisation), or they may conduct it after they have been in the organisation for a few years (with an inside-out view of the organisation).

Common experience shows that salespeople will usually accept an additional non-sales task if the objective is to improve customer experience, and SWOT analyses that contribute to building a productive work environment will certainly accomplish this. While the sales department's SWOT perspective is essential, so are SWOT analyses from other departments. The SWOT analysis is used to identify the organisations internal (Strengths and Weaknesses) and external key factors (Opportunities and Threats) to achieve a specific objective. Below is a simple example of a SWOT analysis (inside-out view) coming from a salesperson.

<u>STRENGTHS</u>

- **Brand**: Well-established company and a trusted brand with a business model that supports its business objectives.
- **Financials**: Continued growth performance.
- **Team**: mutual strengths in software and hardware development with an agile approach to innovation and technology developments.
- **Operations**: efficient supply chain and distribution system.
- **Customer Experience**: Quick and reliable service with a large customer base in the automation sector.

<u>WEAKNESS</u>

- **Employee turnover:** employees are overworked.
- **Low margins:** good cashflow but margins remain low due to errors.
- **Tools**: lack of adequate tools to get deep insights into customer behaviour.
- **Sustainability**: a history of not moving quick enough to sustainable solu-

tions.

- **Accessibility**: We lack the ability to develop genuine access to the right customers and business partners.

OPPORTUNITIES

- **Business Model:** transform a product-based business model into a service-based business model.
- **Expansion**: growth opportunities exist in developing markets like Asia.
- **Partnership**: strategic partner diversification in untapped markets.
- **Approval Process:** Focus on automation in pricing approval and bidding processes.
- **Sales Engagement Process**: improve sales efficiencies and processes to grow top accounts SOW.

THREATS

- **Competition**: competitive industry with both local and global players.
- **Regulations**: difficult to get a clear sense of regulations and policies to uphold in developing countries.
- **Communication**: Deficient communication affects synergy leading to uncertainty, internal competition and power struggle.
- **Corporate Culture**: acceptance rate of business optimisation initiatives might be quicker while transformational adoption is slower.

After the SWOT analysis, the leader may examine the results to identify patterns. Some will become a priority to address as they can bring quick wins for many employees in different parts of the organisation. However, many salespeople have identified specific patterns behind a sales revenue decline. For example, patterns appear when they assess lost deals, or postponements of customer projects, delayed product launches, or the lack of technological enhancements or tools and much more.

The effort you spend as a salesperson to conduct a SWOT or root cause analysis can provide insights and perspectives to guide the decision-making process and reveal implicit knowledge about the organisation. These analyses uncover lessons learned, and the knowledge acquired through them can be used to develop fishbone diagrams showing the cause of specific events that impact the bottom line. All this enables the business to plan and operate more efficiently. By periodically conducting a SWOT analysis (or root cause analysis) or working on fishbone diagrams, the organisation can examine several aspects of its operational excellence and how departments engage in the sales cycle. This activity can identify specific challenges and gather documentation for best-practice methods and approaches.

Tools for the Sales Job

Today, providing a good product is no longer enough. Organisations are continuously finding creative ways to beat the fierce competition. They want to attract new customers and maintain customer loyalty while reducing costs.

While some of what has been described are B2B sales processes and B2B sales techniques, you also require the right B2B sales tools to make much of this happen.

The age of digitalisation has enabled organisations to digitised many of their operations and processes. Also, it has enabled organisations to gather an impressive amount of customer data. The volume of information available online to predict future customer behaviour is now accessible with the click of a button. Fact is that AI knows everything about us, inside and out, and this persuasive technology can affect real-world behaviour and emotions without triggering our awareness.

Similar persuasive technologies are found in sales automation software, and artificial intelligence (AI) sales assistants tools called CRM (Customer relationship management). CRM tools are leveraged by sales and other teams to automate routine tasks and free up time to better prioritise the salesperson's KPI responsibilities. Automation and intelligence algorithms will continue to bring value to organisations and sales professionals to segment customers effortlessly based on their purchase behaviour, demographics, and desires. Consequently, organisations will leverage these assets to create productive business development strategies designed for a specific customer segment and to streamline their processes.

No matter what business sector or organisation size, CRM tools bring a level of logic and standardisation to the sales process that humans can't match. It's no longer a question of when to invest in CRM tools but how to invest in them to accommodate a productive sales workforce.

CRM tools accelerate and enhance the sales process; it eliminates back-end tasks for sales and other teams, enabling them to dedicate more time and resources to closing deals. When organisations have a smart lead qualification system in place, their salespeople can extract valuable data of potential prospects (or customers) with good chances of closing a deal versus opportunities that are not worth pursuing; thus, they shorten the sales cycle and are more conscious of their organisation's expenses and resources. This is where the emergence of CRM tool becomes a moderate personal sales coach with the ability to offer guidance in taking the right actions at the right time to close deals more efficiently.

CRM tools can extract and analyse real-time data to help tailor communication based on data-driven insights. They help the organisation forge long-lasting win-win relations with customers. These intelligent systems built on machine learning algorithms can learn from experience or historical information as they are provided with more data; effectively improving its capacity to analyse and process data over time. CRM tools improve forecasting, and it can identify opportunities to help organisations perform better and sell more. The significant advantage of CRM tools is it can shortens the sales cycle and automate menial processes to save time and resources. Depending on the practices and procedures from one organisation to the other or from one sales activity to another, some of these tasks can widely vary from lead generation with follow-up actions, marketing campaigns with follow-up call activities, weekly sales activities and reporting, to sales pipeline management and accurate forecasting, to data entry, and the scheduling of customer meetings.

The reason some salespeople struggle to convert identified leads into sales can be due to the use of ineffective business intelligence practices. But with a CRM tool, much of this heavy lifting is taken away, providing automated pre-sales operations for all types of non-sales activities for the salesperson. When managing high volumes of leads and prospects where some may slip away, CRM tools actively monitor leads, triggers events, and alerts salespeople when they need to take action. CRM advanced automation tools (or AI-based CRMs) built on machine learning is complementary to this automation process as it completes activities requiring specific competencies that were once considered exclusive to humans. These capabilities include recognising and interpreting data patterns, predicting outcomes, learning from experience rather than being categorically programmed, or interacting using human speech synthesis and recognition. AI-based CRMs can connect data from a variety of domains, analyses data quickly, acts on awareness, and calibrates activities based on past successes and setbacks.

As CRM tools evolve and continue to analyse data to determine its best course of action, it will grow alongside the organisation's operations and salesperson, thus creating a seamless partnership that practically guarantees success. CRM tools will continue to help businesses; analyse customer and prospect data, predict prospects where sales are most likely to win new deals, recommend the critical sales actions to take or prospects to target next, extract relevant forecast parameters using historical data to inform on future results, help leaders forecast their sales team performance for the quarter well in advance, salespeople can opt-in emails to optimise marketing campaigns. It's also a database with customer history information (e.g. future projects, challenges they face, etc.) gathered by the salesperson during the interaction with the customer, and noticeably many more features and functionalities. CRM tools alleviate the sales team of the routine admin-workflows burden, which is now senseless and resource-draining for sales to become more productive, and successful in closing more deals per given annum.

Customers will continue to appreciate automation for everyday purchases, but for complex end-to-end B2B solutions, the customer will require assistance from the salesperson's who leverages activities through the CRM tool. Regardless of how advanced CRM tools become, it will remain a challenge to replace B2B salespeople who make a personal connection with customers and prospects. Though sales automation software and AI sales assistant tools are separate tools, implementing both in tandem brings additional advantages over the competition and allows processes to be optimised. Therefore, when selecting a suitable CRM tool, the CRM consultant will first need to assess a customer's specific situation and demand. This allows the consultant to understand what the customer is hoping the CRM will solve. Because a CRM tool might not even be the right solution to solve a pressing problem, or it might be part of many other initiatives needed to solve an urgent strategic organisational matter.

Many CRM tools exist that can help you manage and monitor all aspects of your business, no matter what size business you operate. It can help you strengthen customer loyalty by knowing more about them and how best to interact with them. This book doesn't recommend specific CRM tools because the organisation usually defines them, but if your organisation has yet to start using CRM tools, you're missing out a vital success factor. CRM tools can change your business for the better, helping you and your employees make better use of your resources.

Chapter 13

Key Performance Indicators

KPI's (Key Performance Indicators) are quantifiable measures used to evaluate the success of an organisation, employee or even an athlete in meeting objectives for performance. It's a valuable management tool designed to measure business performance on an on-going and regular basis of the business planning and management process. So, it's critical that the salesperson understands their KPI's.

In essence, salespeople's KPI's are usually to:

- Achieve sales target quotas.
- Establish and develop a healthy sales pipeline.
- Make customers happy.

Sales and business development can be complicated, intertwined with behavioural and psychological concepts. Also, as the B2B sales cycles shorten and business opportunities become ever complex, B2B sales training programmes have grown in importance. In particular, in the last two decades where innovation and technology are facilitating automation in which specific products sales cycles can bypass the salesperson entirely. Consequently, organisations will continue to seize opportunities to share resources and achieve increased profitability as people continue to buy more products online, and it's less labour intensive and cheaper.

No matter where you sell your products or what you sell, every one of your customers is an individual and deserves to be treated as such. To position your offering as a newly hired salesperson, you should break the market down into smaller segments of specific target audiences: buyers with shared traits, demographics, lifestyles, spending habits, characteristics, and other requirements. Whether you have fifty large customers or a hundred small ones, you need to develop different customer segments. In prioritising customer segments, salespeople usually consider the 80/20 rule, meaning 20% of customers generate 80% of the sales revenue. Also, 100% of all new customer acquisition revenue comes from 20% of your sales team.

For that reason, many salespeople first set priorities for the top customers who account for 80% of their revenue targets to achieve because, in too many organisations, there are not enough resources allocated to the salesperson's region to develop the remaining 20% of customers further. Even so, this 80/20 prioritisation rule usually results in salespeople overachieving their targets since they're better able to work with the customer segments that deliver more valuable results. Once they understand and complete the customer segmentation, many salespeople then consider an account plan as the next steps for their top customers. Account planning in a world of sales is to understand the customer's perspective and complement it with your product and expertise acquired from comparable customers, thus creating a competitive advantage.

Putting your efforts into the wrong customer segment can be time-consuming and expensive to manage and maintain. Therefore, try to stay away from customers with low potentials to buy, that are not financially strong or who seem to be only interested in bargaining rates. Staying away from these customer segments and focusing on better ones will increase margins, improve your SOW for those customer segments and create stability in your customer base. For example, let's imagine a salesperson has 100 customers and breaks them down into smaller target audiences with specific activities to accommodate them.

Though each organisation differs in how they conduct account planning, the following examples of customer segments and activities can be a possible approach to account planning:

Customer A (Urgent) - Tier 1 Accounts

You prioritise Tier 1 accounts according to potential and SOW opportunity growth. The objective here is to:

- Retain & Develop Tier 1 accounts.
- Implement account planning on selective top tier 1 accounts (e.g. Quarterly governance meeting, delivery performance results, technical cases resolved, pricing refresh, provide NDA's for product lifecycle management and product roadmap information, etc.).
- Strengthen relation (e.g. plan workshops, provide research data or customer surveys results, organise marketing activities or loyalty programs and customers events).
- Improve NPS / customer satisfaction (e.g. ensure adequate escalation management, operational excellence, customer service, technical support, product support, order/data management, CRM data entry and forecasting).
- Salespersons response time for tier 1 accounts can be 4-8hrs.
- Two visits a month is more than sufficient.

Customer B (Important) - Tier 2 Accounts

You prioritise tier 2 accounts according to potential product up-sell and cross-sell opportunities by:

- Growing the account to become a tier 1 customer by focusing on product up-sell & cross-sell business opportunities.
- Strengthen relation (e.g. ensure adequate escalation management to grow customer satisfaction, provide market trend information and customer reference insights, etc.).
- Connect to their needs and set priorities for lead generation (e.g. customer events, product demos and workshops, marketing campaigns and target promotion, loyalty programs, strategic alliances, CRM data management and forecasting).
- Salespersons response time for tier 2 accounts can be 6-12hrs.
- A monthly customer visits at a minimum.

Customer C (Retain and Develop) - Tier 3 Accounts

You prioritise tier 3 accounts according to potential product mix opportunities and business strategy alignment by:

- Growing them to become tier 2 accounts.
- Telemarketing (e.g. cold calling, provide referrals and plan lead generation and marketing activities, etc.).
- RFP customers, one-shot projects.
- Salespersons response time for tier 3 accounts can be 8-16hrs.
- A monthly customer visits at a maximum.

According to a 2016 survey by Altify, an account planning strategy contributes to an organisations' bottom line. The following are the research results with 1,034 participants working for 942 companies in 62 countries:

- 72% of participants cited an increased understanding of a customer's business as one of the critical benefits of account planning.
- 74% of participants cited a better win rate.
- 56% of participants cited better customer loyalty.

The account plan is a process that serves high-profile customers. It's usually done in collaboration with the customer who sets annual objectives for the salesperson's organisation. For example, an objective could be to improve the NPS (Net Promoter Score) with a quicker response and reaction time or to reduce costs, or even to ensure the completion of an installation within a given timeframe. These objectives are then reviewed and approved by both organisation's leadership teams who then review progress and recalibrate the account plan on a quarterly or biannual basis. In some cases, the salesperson's bonus structure is aligned to the account plan KPIs. Account planning is key to efficient business development, but many salespeople and too many leaders ignore it or do it without a clear purpose. Without an account plan, salespeople will be challenged to earn trust with top customers.

The more energy you devote to your customer relationships, the higher your retention rate. The rationale is simple; keeping a loyal customer is much cheaper than acquiring a new one. Plus, loyal customers help grow your customer base organically as referrals or through word of mouth. Furthermore, every customer you lose is another negative opinion you will be forced to overcome, respectively, another customer you will need to replace. Numbers don't lie, and since change is constant, whereas business development is optional, you will need to practice setting priorities straight through account planning along with calibrating activities to achieve those critical sales quotas and KPI factors.

Your First Day on the New Sales Job

It's usually evident that the organisation who hires a new salesperson expects its future to be better than the past. In other words, their status quo may have become less innovative to protect revenues and margins streams. The organisation may now envision a new journey of continuous growth rather than a continuation of the past. They may want the salesperson to help the organisation respond quickly to changing business needs and demands. The organisation may also plan to reduce costs by leveraging best-practice methods for sales optimisation, improving service delivery and operational excellence, taking into account the regional and local needs.

The first day on the new job may be among the most memorable and perhaps the most stressful since you don't know what to expect in the new workplace. Even the managers of new hires are sometimes unclear about what is expected. This may be due to vague definitions that provide no detailed understanding of how each co-worker's role engages with the others. The vagueness can also lead to a disconnection between departments within the organisation. Even when roles and processes were once well-defined, they might no longer be relevant or sustainable as the marketplace and customer demands evolve.

Though a leader aims to construct a productive workforce where employees are engaged, don't assume the organisation has one when you start a new role. An unproductive workplace may happen due to co-workers having all sorts of expectations of a salespersons R&R (roles & responsibilities) or due to many still not recognising what precisely sets a salesperson apart from other parts of the organisation, or they don't quite understand what a salesperson's KPIs are. As a result, salespeople may be given various non-sales activities as the workload gets pushed back to the sales department.

Remember that salespeople are expensive resources, and they are one of the only departments that directly generate revenue; thus, it's not only a cost centre. Salespeople have to carry a heavy load during every financial year, and they are not in finance, human resources, engineering, product management, project management, or operations; they are salespeople paid to generate revenue and need to grow profits by reaching out to customers and prospects. Therefore, their KPIs should be the organisation's top priority, and this understanding should reflect on the way the organisation allocates adequate resources to do their sales job smoothly.

For that reason, high sales performers at successful organisations move quickly — not recklessly, but with a sense of urgency. Their efficiency is motivated by the revenue targets a salesperson should deliver annually. Something no other department in an organisation will experience or can relate too. Say what you will about a salesperson or their responsibilities, but their unique strengths are precisely what makes them crucial for any organisation. It may sound obvious to many, but one would be surprised at how many R&R a salesperson may have that has nothing to do with their KPI's. In the end, salespeople need to make sales and will be measured by their annual results where their performance is usually judged by the following:

- What was the salesperson's year-on-year (YoY) revenue growth?
- What was the salesperson's overall share-of-wallet growth with top customers?
- How many new product deals were closed, or new customers acquired in that financial year?
- How healthy is the sales pipeline growth year-on-year (YoY)?
- How many unhappy customers did the salesperson turn around?

Apart from the KPI's and co-workers having all sorts of expectations from salespeople, another challenge they face is that people have an opinion about salespeople, which is often negative, and unfortunately, they continue to be viewed inaccurately. Too many people view salespeople as sleazy, dishonest or they have the impression of salespeople as "know-it-alls". Everyone has strengths and weaknesses, and the best team players bring valuable expertise to the table when they share their lessons learned and expertise with others. Yet when a salesperson demonstrates what they know, others may interpret this as a superiority complex; they see the sales expert as arrogant and withdraw their engagement due to a misconception.

However, the majority of salespeople are committed who want the best for their organisation and the wellbeing of their customers. The salesperson's urgency to achieve their annual KPIs may appear arrogant or self-serving, but salespeople are experts in best-practice sales methods and were hired to do their best at what they do well, which is closing deals. Remember that rarely do other departments of an organisation have annual KPIs to achieve. For salespeople to be considered productive and not arrogant, the organisation should ensure all their employees clearly understand that when the salesperson (a high cost resource) is occupied with non-sales activities, this will detract them from the organisation's ability to achieve its bottom-line growth targets.

Considering all these factors, salespeople need to have thick skin or learn to grow some in the world of sales and business development and be willing to be criticised on the quality of work and their results. Salespeople's stress amongst others stems from:

- The need to meet annual quotas.
- The balancing act of managing short-term objectives to achieve long-term goals.
- Having little control (or none) over the rest of their organisation's ability to deliver a positive customer experience to ensure pre-sales and post-sales engagement processes are effective and continuously followed.
- Lack of innovation and inclusion into business optimisation initiatives to shorten the sales cycle or specific parts of it, such as product time-to-market.
- Not having the right tools and resources for the job.
- The fierce competition in the marketplace.

However, when salespeople can develop a sense of fearlessness and program-specific disciplines for facing challenges head-on, these discouragements will lose their power.

Mastering best-practice habits and becoming fearless in the face of rejection will also prepare a salesperson to become a leader or entrepreneur later on. So, if you are ambitious to become the next Warren Buffett (paperboy), Howard Schultz (salesman), or Mark Cuban (software salesperson), you should learn how to sell and position both your products and yourself. Regardless of what you sell or where you sell in the world, the one most crucial points to remember is that you should protect your personal brand since this is what you carry to the next stage of your career. Here, the corporate culture of your organisation can have a make-or-break impact. That said, when entering a new job situation, salespeople usually focus on:

- Building rapport with co-workers, especially the people you will be working closely with each day. Learn to know them on a personal level – ask questions and share details about yourself.
- Getting a clear understanding of the way things work within the organisation. The first few weeks of a new job are mostly consumed with meetings and induction training. Listen to learn and ask questions about the people, products, process, practices, and policies.
- Getting to know your manager's approach – everyone has a different management style. Since the manager and employee relationship is directly linked to the organisation's productivity, which you cannot change, it is ever so important to learn and understand your manager's way of doing things.
- Learning the corporate culture. This is usually an implied practice, not expressly defined. You'll learn the ins and outs by seeing it in action among your co-workers. The corporate culture in a large organisation can sometimes be challenging, but most of the time, it turns out to be a tremendous life-learning experience and a privilege working with these fantastic co-workers that collaborate to promote inclusion as they conduct themselves bravely against the competition.
- Identifying the key players in your organisation. Impressing your boss is one

challenge, but you should also try to identify other key players with influence in the organisation. Both your manager and these leaders can make or break your chances of getting a raise or promotion. Getting to know them allows you to make a lasting impression.

- Practicing due diligence – do the best at your job every day towards achieving your KPIs while complying with all applicable guidelines and the organisation's code of conduct. When there isn't a clear rule, pick common sense as your guide for integrity.

The following steps can help salespeople assess and gather adequate business intelligence to ensure the organisation is and remains healthy:

- Current status when hired: Among others, an organisation should provide new hires adequate information on the health of the organisation. This could be their customer segments, sales pipeline, current or future business opportunities and projects, success factors and challenges in their region, and information on the different platforms to join when bidding for tenders. Such workplace-knowledge transfer should be handed over to new employees by their predecessor during an induction training programme with guidance on how to make the best use of the organisation's available resources and technology. Proper handovers for new hires will shorten the time it takes for them to understand the business and hit the ground running with confidence.
- The short-term is to discover opportunities. For instance, the salesperson can use the first month to learn the CRM or ERP tool to extract customer order history from past years - three years' order history could provide an even stronger pattern. This provides useful information and helps the salesperson understand what strategic action to take to grow business or prevent loss.
- The mid-term objective is to learn the ins and outs of the workplace and assess the organisation's operational excellence. In the first few months, speak to as many employees as possible. If any, even employees of other affiliated brands within the group, to build rapport and understand the bigger picture.
- The long-term objective is to evaluate the productivity of the organisation's corporate culture. After twenty-four months on the job, salespeople can identify a revenue benchmark they could achieve for their assigned sales region. Using this benchmark, salespeople can then quantify the revenue performance impact of the health of the corporate culture by identifying patterns of employee disengagement or flawed operational excellence. These are correlated to revenue results in a way that can be calculated by considering employee salary costs, delayed project implementation revenues, potential lost deals, and missed sales revenues. For example, when a deal is won, but the project installation is delayed due to project management issues or severe structural flaws in operational excellence in the post-sales phase. Here,

> the salesperson can estimate these impacts from their regional sales revenue benchmark to determine the overall value of missed (or delayed) revenues and margin for that financial year. These calculations may result in extraordinary figures, considering that it only comes from a business development perspective. That is why a productive corporate culture is a vital success factor for any business development strategy, which is, in turn, a critical differentiating factor for the bottom-line success or failure of an organisation.

As a salesperson starting a new job, you can either begin to create a sales strategy or continue with your predecessor's as you learn it. Most organisations have not radically changed their strategies for years. Instead, changes to strategies are incremental, building from one year to the next. Many organisations attempt to get better at what they already do well, always hoping that no competitor comes along with a fresh idea which wipes out their business model. That said, whenever you want to influence an organisational strategy, you should research and reflect on and consider the pre-configured strategic goals of the organisation, their tools and practices used to achieve their goal.

Most businesses prefer incremental strategies due to the low risk they present in comparison to reinventing a strategy – which is risky unless this new strategy has buy-in from all stakeholders and will guarantee a minimum growth value. A successful strategy always comes down to what solution will solve a pressing need or problem in a sustainable, economically viable way that is made hard to be emulated by new entrances or competitors. Whether you are a start-up entrepreneur or a salesperson trying to increase your revenue performance, begin by creating a business development strategy within the first few months on the new job, stick to that plan and then return to this strategy for re-evaluation every financial year.

Chapter 14

Sales Engagement Preparation Plan

The Preparation Plan

The preparation plan (Research and Prepare for customer interactions) is a practice that will dramatically improve the efficiency of your sales activities simply by keeping track of what you want to achieve during each customer interaction. With it, you will interact more purposefully with customers and prospects.

The preparation plan is a document and practice used for meetings in the sales cycle. It doesn't require complete sentences; you can outline pertinent information using bullet points, short phrases, or numbers. The preparation plan could be in the form of an Excel table or word document that incorporates the following sections:

- Customer information - Who will you meet (title and contact details of attendees)?
- Agenda - What are the meeting objectives?
- Opening statement - How will you open the discussion?
- Build rapport - What value can your organisation show that can complement the customer's actual situation? What will you say or do to address their key beliefs?
- Questions - What questions do you want to ask the customer? What questions might the customer ask you, and how will you respond to them?
- Objections - How will you respond to customer's objections about your offering or about your organisation?
- Next steps - What action (if any) will you and the customer each take next?

As you develop your preparation plan, you will draw upon your intellect to structure the upcoming interaction in ways that benefit both you and the customer. As you execute your preparation plan, you will rely on your EQ (emotional intelligence - quotient) to determine what you will say to the customer. EQ measures your ability to recognize your emotions, the emotions of others, and their effects.

In the preparation plan phase, salespeople need information on the customer that includes: their purchase history, their key players and decision-making process, the business sector they sell in, information on the customer's competitors, and their estimated annual budget, along with any other information relevant to their business success. This allows the salesperson to get the big picture and use the insights gathered to build rapport further.

Whether you are approaching a small, medium or large organisation, you'll need first to research to get useful insights. Finding the information necessary to fill out your preparation plan, as described in this chapter, is a good start. Generally, this will require a combination of quantitative and qualitative research in which both primary sources (information published by your customers' organisation and its end customers) and secondary ones (industry reports and other information from third parties or about their competitors) have been considered. You can research on the web, reading social media content, blogs, newsletters and in particular, news websites help identify business leads. For example, suppose a salesperson who sells fire alarms or fire extinguishers reads about a massive fire in a building, the salesperson could test and follow-up on this potential lead by contacting the facility manager and mapping out how their solution can mitigate future risks of fire.

Customers have access to more information than ever before, and so do you. Therefore, before an interaction begins, know the customer's organisation and what they do. Also, you need to know as much information as possible about the individual with whom you will interact. Building rapport with customers seems obvious, but when was the last time you spoke to an existing customer or a potential prospect? Existing customers are a perfect source of information since they've already purchased your solutions and are relatively accessible. Interviewing them offers tremendous insight into their organisation and operations, including the gathering of information to why they like working with your organisation is valuable.

The goal is to identify common ground and the challenges the customer faces. Customers and prospects are always on the lookout for an alternative supplier to their incumbent, and they could be willing to meet a potential partner that can offer different approaches in solving the challenges they face and if the alternative supplier's salesperson is trustworthy.

Study your competitor's testimonials from their customers to understand why a customer awarded your competitor business over you in the past. Also, on your competitor's websites, you may find their partner list. From this list, consider who you could contact to develop a strategic alliance with to enter into untapped markets. Try to leverage professional networks and your social media presence to identify industry-specific platforms where your prospects might be. These networks are great for engaging with potential customers and will help you get a better understanding of the challenges they face and the success factors they will need. This interaction allows you to ask questions, receive detailed and thoughtful responses that will enhance the data you already have at hand.

In every customer interaction, the salesperson ought to take notes of what they have learned, including observations on the customer's challenges, concerns, and priorities for the coming years. When you take notes, you create a meeting report that will help determine if a specific customer should be a salesperson's priority or not. Meeting reports are a critical aspect of information gathering that many salespeople forget to dispatch. After the meeting, you should create a follow-up email for the customer. This is when you can attach a meeting report on the topics discussed and the agreed-upon next steps. Customer meeting reports can be long and detailed, or short and to the point, depending on the nature of the meeting. Where the meeting is important, you might need to make a detailed meeting report while in a less critical meeting, one can have a list of decisions made and the next steps required to take with the customer. Salespeople should disseminate customer meeting reports 24-48 hours after the meeting, and this information gathered from the meeting can be inserted into the CRM tool. Since not all organisations have a CRM tool in place, the meeting report can be in the form of a word document incorporating the following:

- Where did the meeting take place (date and time) and who were the participants (title and contact details)
- Conclusion of the meeting outcome (meeting agenda and objective):
    - Was the first meeting objective achieved?
    - Was the second meeting objective achieved?
- Leads identified (If any, what potential leads did you identify or qualify?)
- Other information gathered (What new and essential information did you learn?)
- Next steps:
    - What will you and the customer do next?
    - Other essentials – as mentioned, when required, send the meeting report to the customer for their review and archive it in the CRM tool (when available).

The main purpose of meeting reports is to share customer information within your organisation. The meeting report also becomes your guide, to drive actions, to make decisions, to identify customer behavioural patterns, to create a product in demand, to build relations and to inform others. Most importantly, it helps your organisation increase its value through a database of customer information, thus also making the handovers for new hires being equipped to perform straight away with valuable customer insights.

Customer information is worth its weight in gold, and it needs to be treated as such, but this rarely happens — this occurs due to departments working separately from each other and dealing with customers in different ways. Consequently, employees may even keep customer information to themselves, as opposed to sharing it with other departments. Sharing customer information creates a productive internal collaboration to troubleshoot an issue better, resulting in increased customer experience. Successful organisations and salespeople understand the importance of sharing customer information and in having insight into potential customer behaviour. Therefore, do the right job and keep communication levels high on customer information even though other departments might not be keen on sharing essential customer information.

During the research and preparation phase for customer interactions, you will reach a point where you have gathered enough insight to have some value you can deliver to the customers. Customers (or prospects) appreciate receiving information on industry-specific statistics, information about their completion, market trends, or industry challenges. Also, details about your organisation and the solutions you offer: product launch announcements, the fact that a product is going EOL (end-of-life), new service or product offerings. It's a quid pro quo game, in which your committed engagement with customers can be rewarding. Customers won't forget the salesperson who helped to solve their pressing issues, although this still doesn't guarantee that the customer will purchase something again. Yet, you should assume that your competitors are never at rest, so never take an acquired customer for granted.

The fruits of your research and generosity towards customers are part of your job along with your close ratio being impacted by the knowledge you gather. And the more you use the preparation plan model, the easier they become to develop. You'll find your customer meetings will become more productive and will proceed more logically. Your sales cycle will shorten because business opportunities will flow more quickly through your sale pipeline. This creates better momentum in winning new deals and delivering better revenue results. All of these aspects become part of your "brand". Business developers and salespeople know that their brand is of great importance as it is their track record that will follow them wherever they go. Your brand as a salesperson must be sacred to you — so protect it and get to know your brand value. In fact, the salesperson's brand is all they have. The personal brand theory in the context of a business developer and salesperson goes: "Your positive mental attitude is your logo. Your adaptive social style is your business card; how others experience your engagement is your trademark. All these together create your brand. Learn to become a salesperson who develops their brand to leave a legacy behind."

The preparation plan can also be useful when planning for an interview. Fact is that employee turnover is unavoidable, and people are always on the hunt for the next big opportunity, especially in the digital age, we face extremely short job tenure where employees are likely to hold upwards of ten jobs throughout their career. Therefore, organisations that have no employee retention plan for employees who aren't content or fulfilled at their current job might continue to experience the increase in employee turnover.

Customers' Decision-Making Process

Getting the customer to tell you about their internal decision-making process is the biggest challenge when building rapport in the sales cycle. No one is willing to share sensitive information about their organisation, and rightly so. Additionally, even when it comes to more general information that could still be helpful to you, many people you encounter might not understand their organisation's entire decision-making process and all the players involved. Therefore, a salesperson should speak with as many people in different parts of the customer's organisation to get the complete picture of who is involved in the decision-making process.

You can develop a schema of the customer's decision-making process that incorporates the following:

- What steps does the customer take during the entire purchase process?
- Who is involved in each step of the decision-making process?
- What kinds of decisions are made at each step?
- When will each decision be made?
- What criteria and beliefs are essential for each individual decision-maker?
- What is their estimated budget for that potential business lead you are qualifying?

It is key to remember that most of your potential customers are happy with what they have otherwise, they would have already contacted you long ago. Therefore, the quicker a salesperson learns how the customer's decision-making process works, the sooner they will begin working with the right people, thereby shortening the sales cycle. On the other hand, the number of people you have to identify as part of this decision-making process may vary from two up to twenty, depending on the organisation size. In this scenario, it's helpful during the entire sales cycle not to rush this preparation. Speak with as many contacts as possible at a customer's site. This will also offer an excellent chance to get to know their social styles discussed in chapter 9 (Architypes In Perspective). Also, the organisational chart that is sometimes available on the organisations' website or elsewhere on the web can help during the preparation process in finding out more about the people you plan to meet.

Regardless of which market you sell in, the size of the customer's organisation you approach, or their business model and other factors, the final decision a customer makes ultimately has to do with trust. When trust is high, even a higher proposal price may still not sway them in your competitor's direction. You are more likely to get the contract awarded if you have committed yourself to build rapport with many people throughout the organisation as you accommodate their interests and different social styles during and after the sales cycle. Don't view this as mere socialising or a waste of time — but to ensure you have enough time to spend on this task, look for the opportunity for efficiencies throughout the sales cycle, and keep organised with a plan.

Since the salesperson is one of the organisations' most expensive resources, they should spend their time economically and work with SMART objectives (specific, measurable, achievable, realistic, and timely) to achieve their KPI goals.

Chapter 15

Effective Communication is Active Listening

Turning to the essential part of sales is effective communication, whether verbal, nonverbal or written, transmit your expertise and confidence to others. From the way we choose to dress to the speed and tone of our voice, our facial expression and body gestures, and our vocabulary, we are directly or indirectly sending out signals all the time to those around us. People know that to resolve uncertainties and disagreements, we need to communicate, but negative communication patterns can often lead to more significant frustration and escalation of conflicts.

We have all faced the most emotional aspects of our communication in perceiving and interpreting the world and reality around us. This comes from our experience, education, our relationship with others and our personalities that may lead us to stereotype assumptions of others whose backgrounds differ from our own. In this case, one might be tempted to hide behind the impersonal forms of communication offered by technology to avoid eye contact and the immediacy of the spoken word. For all the efficiencies of digital communication available today, a phone call or face-to-face meeting remains a genuine human interaction. For some people in certain circumstances, however, this genuineness can feel threatening.

Dealing with conflict impacts our physical, emotional, and mental health. However, the negative impact can be lessened with more productive ways of handling the conflict. It's worth learning and implementing particular communication skills that will improve your interactions with others. Communication is essential for any relationship, even for a temporary transaction between individuals. Being human means communicating every second, consciously or subconsciously. Two essential things to understand about communication, especially in the workplace, are (i) it's vital to read situations so as to determine what response is required, and (ii) excessive workload and pressure can ultimately lead us to lose sight of the need to communicate.

Effective communication in a group setting is not only what you say, how you say it, or what you do; it also includes awareness of what other group members can contribute to the interaction. It's through practical communication skills that a group can work harmoniously, effectively, and productively. With fruitful communication, group members can engage in productive debates and contribute their experience to successful meetings. Being well-spoken puts you in a much stronger position to proficiently, fluently, and tactfully articulate a situation. Think of your voice as an instrument and your communication style as the melody. When used effectively, it can convey your message and engage your audience.

Listen to those around you. For instance, when someone uses demeaning language while communicating with others, such demining language indicates the relationship exists on a lack of mutual respect. On the contrary, someone using a language associated with receptiveness will be communicating in a relationship based on mutual respect within a hierarchy of one's position of authority and responsibility. Therefore, greater awareness of other's language usage can help you become more conscious of your language usage.

Any change begins with awareness, and you cannot improve what you cannot hear. Nonverbal communication allows you to read and use body language to build better personal and professional relationships. These nonverbal signals can give additional information and meaning over and above the spoken communication. Some estimates suggest that up to 80% of communication is nonverbal. Nonverbal communication includes eye contact, tone of voice, facial expressions, posture or body movement. Therefore, learn how to become sensitive by identifying the nonverbal signals.

The most effective communication is uncomplicated, concise, direct, and honest. Treat your speech like a conversation, with room for input from other people. Be sure you're either telling your audience something they don't know or helping them identify an important point they need to remember. Also, remember that our thinking speed is about 500 words a minute, much faster than anyone can talk or listen. Furthermore, the natural parts of our minds will sometimes also move on to other topics in a long conversation, but we must resist this temptation. Keep in the present moment and don't let your mind wander off only to dart back to the conversation. Use the time to your advantage by listening to and interpreting the nonverbal messages.

It can help to repeat the core idea several times in a slightly varied form so that your listeners become more confident that they understand your intended message. You are also more likely to get your point across by announcing your message in a chronological structure at the beginning by laying out your information in a straightforward manner so that listeners can quickly process it. Being clear about the message means your audience won't have to fight confusion. For example, when you begin a presentation, you could say, the presentation has three key elements:

- First, I'll describe the purpose of the survey.
- Second, we'll review the evaluation criteria.
- And third, we'll examine the survey results.

The listener now knows what to expect. Think of your audience as guests. The more you plan with this in mind, the happier your audience will be. Keep their patience, interest, and curiosity at the forefront of your objective.

In addition, it should become a habit developing the awareness of superlatives (oldest) or intensifiers (very), along with empty words and phrases such as "you know" or "uh" or "um" leaking into your conversation. The first step in transforming your vocabulary habits is to select one word you want to deal with to make it more meaningful. Superlatives and intensifiers certainly have places in our daily communication, yet the less we use them, the more meaningful they become. When something relatively common can get you to use the word "oldest" or "best", it seems to indicate that your experience is limited. So, what is one word you want to make sure you're not overusing? The second step is paying attention when you say the word during a conversation. Practice saying the same sentence, but this time use another word. The third step is sensitising yourself to the word so that you become aware of intending to use it before it even happens.

When you understand that it's not only what you say but how you say things, you become more able to avoid communication-blockage behaviours. These can include repetition or imprecision, and also attitudes such as ordering someone to do something rather than suggesting it. To become a powerful speaker, in public or one-on-one, remain genuine and comfortable with your audience and:

- Arrive early at the event to mingle with some of the audience and make sure the technology is ready for your presentation.
- Know your audience and get in touch with their thoughts and feelings.
- Know your stories and use them effectively so that your message connects to your audience's interests.
- Know how to reduce and manage your anxiety. Ultimately, this all comes down to how well you have prepared your presentation and yourself for this interaction:
  - Know how you will best focus on your message.
  - Know how you will capture the audience's attention.
  - Know how you will communicate your message with speed, clarity, and effectiveness (for instance, by putting the most important detail first).
  - Know how you will choose the best words for your message – ones that are simple, concrete, and accurate.

A Mindful Presenter

Sales and business development are about dialogue, including attending meetings and giving presentations. Your skill presenting information in a persuasive and engaging way will have enormous potential to move you forward on your career path. The positive impression left behind after a strong presentation performance can pay off big down the road. Strong presentation skills can build your career when you leave a long-lasting impression of being someone who can confidently and professionally handle high-pressure situations that demand clear thinking and clear communication.

Though salespeople are often busy with many tasks, they should find the time to sharpen their presentation skills. Let me mention, this is not a step-by-step guide for developing and delivering presentations, nor is it a step-by-step guide for public speaking and performing. You can find guides to becoming a good public speaking, presenter, and performer elsewhere. I liked the book titled, No Sweat Public Speaking by Fred E. Miller. The information presented in this chapter is to enhance your presenter and presentation skills.

As radical as it may sound, you don't need to have a slide deck all the time. In fact, your presentation will become stronger with a blank screen that redirects the audience's attention back to you. People buy from people and by enhancing your connection with your audience will help you convey your message. When a presenter uses the blank-screen approach, they get their audience's full, undivided attention, and many appreciate its effectiveness. Hence, you want to be a powerful presenter and communicator, not a slideshow master.

However, when getting a team ready for a big presentation, plan as a team. The more talent, creativity, and experience are put into a presentation, the higher the performance results. This is particularly critical in fast-paced organisational environments where limited time is available for preparation and rehearsal. Work out the overall flow as a team and make sure everyone knows what everyone else is developing for the presentation. The outcome is a more integrated presentation that has buy-in from all team members and comes across as a single, unbroken message. Remember, just as a single presenter needs to transition from one slide to the other smoothly, multiple speakers on a team need to transition from one speaker to the next. Each presenter should summarise what they have covered and then link it to what the next speaker is going to cover so that the next presenter can reference the previous presenter by saying something like, "as my colleague just mentioned."

When a team leader (or meeting facilitator) controls the meeting, they can take each question and answer it or direct it to another team member. With enough upfront preparation, it's possible to minimise the break between presenters, staging a presentation that is as seamless for the audience as a Broadway play. Remember that no matter how obvious the benefits of your products are, you still have to communicate them in such a way that your audience will recognise and connect to the information presented. The challenge presenters face is that everyone in your audience may not necessarily see what you believe to be obvious. Some may make a connection, while others may not. Another concern is remembering the content linked to each slide deck. Without a story outline to follow, you can all too easily forget what to say next.

For that reason, when you begin gathering the content for the presentation, you should ask yourself: what do you hope the audience will say if they are asked what your presentation was covering? And as you put your final touches on your presentation, take a step back and consider the larger picture. People usually tend to sell the way they buy. For instance, a person who compares analytical data when purchasing a product will also prioritise analytical data when selling a product. Naturally, the challenge is to be sure your interests and social style do not override the different needs, priorities, cultural orientation, learning preferences, and your audience's benefits.

Further, not all parts of your presentation will be equal, given the primacy effect and the recency effect. The primacy effect is the information given at the beginning of a presentation will be most well remembered. The recency effect is the information given at the end of a presentation (that is, most recent) will be second-best remembered. Information in the middle of the presentation will be less vivid than information at either end of it. Naturally, these effects need to be accounted for to make a meaningful impression into your introduction and conclusion. Weak beginnings or endings contain ideas that are disconnected from the rest of the presentation or irrelevant to your audience. Put yourself in their shoes to ensure you address their needs and share information that is meaningful to them. This ensures they'll remember the parts of your presentation that you most want them to.

Remember that the customer's logo should be visible on your presentation proposal just as their needs are reflected in it. Salespeople learn that the person in the customer's organisation who will view the presentation will finally have to present it to their leaders to get buy-in. By having their logo on your presentations, you help that person become well equipped to present your solution, and their logo in the presentations creates additional value. While you may use a customer's logo in your presentation, copyright/trademark and the implications of using a customer's logo in your marketing materials without their expressed consent can negatively impact your relations with the customer or prospect. Therefore, during the preparation phase of the presentation, you could ask the customer if it's okay to use their logo.

As usual, you need to make a good first impression that captures attention. For example, you can start by opening a presentation on sales performance for instance with a relatable question like, "How many of you have run short on product samples for customers to test in the last month?" Though there is no one right or wrong way to begin your presentation, some salespeople prefer using anecdotes to open. People like stories and salespeople can take advantage of storytelling.

The disconnect that comes from sitting in presentations that take longer than promised is so widespread that the opportunity to make a positive impression by staying on time is tremendous. If factors beyond your control make it likely you'll run overtime, explain to your audience what you still have to cover. Then determine if they have the time and willingness to let you continue. Be willing to gracefully stop and make arrangements to deliver the remaining information to them by other means.

Your audience is going to read you just as surely as they read your slides. They will notice signs of likeability, which may make them more receptive to your message.

They see how and who you talk to and will draw a conclusion about your status. When you exude poise and confidence or act unsure of yourself, they will notice it. The ever-important first impression has been made, and it's influencing your intended message. Your audience members will read phoniness as sure as they read any other message you communicate. You should always be authentic and be constantly considerate that your behaviour is sending out messages. Your public speaking message begins as soon as you are in public and long before you face the audience and make your opening statement. Therefore, try considering the following approaches during presentations:

- When rules have been set at the beginning of the meeting, they help avoid much of the unproductive behaviour. Getting people to think about what is and isn't acceptable behaviour can work wonders. They become conscious of how they need to act as meeting participants and audience members. When necessary, the meeting facilitator can interrupt long enough for a rule reminder, and then the presenter can get right back to where they left off.
- Don't try to deviate from your initial plan. Rather, trust and believe in your preparation plan, and establish a reasonable tone to stick with, even if it takes a while for the audience to start responding positively to it. Naturally, focusing on serving your audience well is far more productive than focusing and commenting on how you can better serve yourself.
- When during your presentation you face an uninspired audience, know that you can usually get ten uninterrupted minutes if you ask for it. These ten minutes are incredibly precious when misunderstanding contributed to the uninspired atmosphere, and you now have the chance to set the record straight and make your case in an organised manner. The best time to deal with troublesome audience members is before they become troublesome. If you can meet with those who you suspect might be disruptive in advance and negotiate a peace treaty, your presentation will go better. For instance, when you know your audience well, ask them about their resistance and try to learn from that. Then diffuse the situation of negative energy in the room by using humour on something or a comment that was said in the room. It's is difficult to be angry and laugh at the same time. So, when they start laughing, you will see the negative energy start to dissipate but remember not to be a comedian. When you face a challenge from your audience, do your best to stay calm and show no signs of defensiveness by focusing on breathing in a few times and releasing your breath without the audience noticing.
- A tranquil reaction reflects well on you and has the bonus value of increasing the audience's confidence in your message. After all, if you are not bothered by an attack, you obviously must believe your message will stand up to criticism. The next time you face an audience member's objections, test how much this person speaks for others. You can do this by asking how many in

the room have the same concern? Insist on knowing who these people are and don't accept without question that they really exist. It is to your advantage no matter which way it goes. You'll have a better understanding of how well your persuasive message is really being conveyed and be able to address the objections of specific people rather than a faceless or unreal mass.

- Weak or angry voices discourage listening. The 100 muscles working in synchronicity to project your voice is impressive, so too is the fact that voice analysis can identify illnesses. If you suspect your voice can use some improvement, a small investment in seeing a voice coach will pay off big. If speaking softly is your chosen voice style, suggesting that you're a kind person, then that is okay. Your voice plays a critical role in determining how successful you are as a presenter as it directly affects how much people listen to you and what image you project. Confidence and enthusiasm are communicated to a great extent by a person's tone of voice and body language. To note though, a characteristics voice tonality of a perceived "angry voice" may not be as a result of anger, but this usually triggers an emotional response in the person perceiving the tonality of having the traits of anger. This is not only a physiological matter but an emotional one too.
- Practice speaking slowly with conviction. If you want your audience to care about something, you have to sound like you care. It should not be an act; rather, you must be talking with real conviction. Try thinking through what you intend to say in its completion before saying it out loud. Try not to speak until you have thought out everything you intend to say. Practice to speak slowly in front of a mirror (or camera), take deep breaths and learn to hold onto your thoughts at the same time. When people learn to breathe in a way that supports their voice, they sound better. Suppose you speak too fast or even think too quickly, making your tongue disconnected from your brain. In that case, a simple trick is to have a bottle of water next to you as you speak and drink from it to create natural pauses. Also, try watching videos of good speakers. Record yourself presenting and see how it measures with a speaker that impressed you.
- You may think you don't have a favourite word, but you do. We all do, and that's fine, except when you overuse it so much that your audience loses their own fondness for it. To get rid of a word or phrase habit, you have to find out what it is and get to the point that you can hear yourself saying it. Awareness is 80% of the battle. Listening to your own voicemail is one technique for gaining this awareness. Write down a list of the words you are hearing too often and consider alternatives. Keeping your vocabulary free of repetitive word usage requires a lifelong commitment. New words and phrase will always be trying to attach themselves to you. Stay alert, and you can catch them before they become engrained in your speech patterns.

- Some training programmes urge speakers to develop several new gestures and rehearse them. The best way to add some variety to your gestures without looking artificial is to do some rough pantomiming. You can start by taking your hands out of your pockets. You might keep your open hands close together, or incrementally lower your hands as you talk about the steady drop in sales revenue growth. This kind of spontaneous gesturing adds to your repertoire of nonverbal communication. Some presenters find that holding something, like a pen, is all they need to instantly feel comfortable with their gestures. Yet this may distract your audience as you unconsciously start playing with the pen. Also, instead of remaining in one place like a tree, take advantage of the available floor space. Move around and add to the dynamic quality of your speaking style. Movement, especially when you approach your audience, is a particularly strong way to project confidence and build a connection. Don't feel you have to stay behind the lectern or remain chained to your laptop.
- It's essential to maintain eye contact if you want to make a strong personal connection. When you finish a presentation, your audience should each feel like you spoke directly with them. Therefore, during your presentation, remember to keep eye contact with the decision-makers, especially when you're responding to objections or concerns they may have about your solution or your organisation. When speaking to a group, look at each person for a few seconds so you can feel the connection and then move on. Regardless of the audience size or the decision-makers attending your presentation, the goal is to make everybody feel like you noticed and spoke to them individually.
- Instead of asking if anyone has a question, ask who has the first question or as mentioned earlier, ask a specific one. This change in the way you ask for questions can avoid both awkward silence and people leaving the room with unanswered questions. The secret to giving a quality answer is first insisting on a quality question. Don't be shy about asking for clarification. Also, here is a place where you don't need to worry about a rigid structure. By its very nature, the answer and question period jump's around within the overall subject matter where questions don't have to flow naturally from what preceded them.

Chapter 16

Cold Calling is Essential

Cold calling plays a crucial role in successful prospecting and developing a sales pipeline of potential business opportunities. No matter how talented you are in sales, nothing happens unless you can get an appointment with a potential prospect. Though online advertisement is the most economical way to develop leads, cold calling remains a critical source to generate quality leads. If you knock on many doors and see enough people, you will eventually get a sale.

Cold calling follows the same approach as a warm calling. The difference in cold calling is calling someone you have had no previous contact with while warm calling is following up on a connection you (or your organisation) have dealt with in the past. You still prioritise by selecting a targeted list of prospects to contact. Make sure you have some good reasons for choosing the prospects on your list. In cold calling, you prepare by researching the organisation and employees to develop a preparation plan described in the previous chapter 14 (Sales Engagement Preparation Plan).

Since you lack a powerful referral of a warm caller, it can serve you well to make greater use of reciprocity. When you ask prospects for their time, make it clear you wish to give them value in return. This illustrates your consideration for what they do. It's sufficient to provide them with a small gift or token ahead of time. The goal of reciprocity is to make it easier for the prospect to respond in kind by giving you some of their time and consideration. The gift doesn't need to be a physical item and remember to comply with your organisation's policies and guidelines here. You might send a short video that describes the challenges organisations face and how your organisation helped them, or you could send useful research or articles that would be of interest to the prospect about their business sector or their competitors. When a prospect values what you send them, they will probably reciprocate by offering you a few minutes of their time. Whether you use reciprocity or not, you will still want a preparation plan to streamline the communication with your prospect during the call and meeting. Also, remember to keep notes with follow-up actions of your calls so you can revert to them when needed.

Apart from breaking the ice with the reciprocity rule, you should remember to use a sales call script for any customer interactions. When you use a cold calling script, you will discover the benefits of working with it, and it teaches you how to be effective in cold calling to grow and evolve as a salesperson.

Cold calling is more challenging today than ever before due to the number of calls it takes to reach a prospect than it did years ago. However, if you have a structured method on approaching cold calling, you can make prospects stay on the line once they answer it.

Writing down a cold calling script and practising it out loud can be beneficial. It will feel awkward at first, especially if you have never used or written sales scripts. Yet this practice will improve your ability to open a call more efficiently and adequately establish expectations of what you intend to accomplish from the call. If your organisation doesn't have sales call scripts, various free templates are found on the web to get started with your first cold calling campaign. No excuses, begin with a cold call script today and make adjustments to it over time as you learn more about what resonates and what doesn't with the prospects you speak with over your first few days of cold calling.

Though different cold calling methods, techniques and script templates exist, in reality, when you make cold calls you:

- Have no fear: Start by recognising rejection as a part of your sales career but don't let that stop you from calling and being confident in your sales pitch.
- Do your research: Research the organisation and people you intend to meet.
- Use a personalised script: Be sure to personalise your cold calling script for each particular prospect. Naturally, the more you rehearse the call script, the less you will spend time with it in the future.
- Know when to call: Though there is no right time to for cold calling, calling on the right day and at the right time can work wonders. Experience shows that salespeople usually make cold calls on Tuesdays to Friday from 10 am or 3 pm.
- Make a good first impression: Make the conversation's content about your prospect, not you and remember to keep your objective in mind.
- Leave a voice message: If you are unable to get through, leave a pre-record voicemails so you can move onto your next call.

Another essential step in the preparation phase for customer interactions is to check in with your prospect on how they would like to run the meeting. Checking in ensures all meeting attendees can commit to the meeting objective and agenda well in advance. When you prerequisite, you want to do four things:

- Agree with your prospect on the meeting's objective.

- Gain approval on the meeting agenda. Both you and your prospect should see that the agenda items are appropriate, comprehensive, and when adequately addressed, will help them agree on a specific course of action.
- Outline what you and the prospect can do before the meeting to arrive well prepared.
- Request any information that you might need in advance to make good use of the time.

You can cover these questions in a phone call or email before the scheduled meeting. We covered the elements of preparing for the sales engagement process in chapter 14, and one is strongly recommended for all-important interactions.

Cold Calling Example

Customers and prospects don't care about who you are or what your organisation does, and probably every salesperson has been in a situation where they became too talkative as they got into a captivating conversation in which they forgot the reason for the call. Remember that the number one reason for your call is to make an appointment, and when necessary, redirect your attention towards that objective. You can continue conversations with your prospect as you build rapport in your future phone calls, emails, video conferences, or face-to-face meetings in an ongoing relationship.

You can use the following cold calling example as a basis to develop your own:
<u>Cold Calling for a meeting request to position a CRM software:</u>

Hello Kate, my name is Peter, and I'm calling from XYZ. I don't know how it is with you, but when speaking to other leaders in the industry, I keep hearing three things. First, revenue and margins aren't growing the way they should or need to. They want adequate tools and analytics to help them correct the situation. Second, they have some sales engagement and productivity issues that need to be addressed: various costs of the salespeople's metrics performance are missing, or worse, salespeople don't have any metrics to identify the real problem. And third, the organisation lacks high-quality business intelligence about their customers, and this is also hurting up-selling and cross-sell initiatives. These elements all affect revenues in profound ways. Have any of these been an issue at your organisation as well?

Curious, I did some research and came across something that might be considered a red flag to many customers. It seems that during the last three years, your SGA [selling, general and administrative] expenses have been running around 10-15% higher than the industry average. Before that, you were aligned or even a little below. That sometimes indicates an underlying sales performance issue or other factors can be at work. Would you be willing to share your thoughts over a lunch meeting on what your reactions are to these numbers, and we don't have to restrict our conversation to this specific topic?

Would one of the following dates suit you (or can you propose dates that work best for you)?

February 12th at 12 noon

February 13th at 12 noon

When you make a daily cold calling goal, your objective should also include a rejection ratio you want to achieve. This rejection ratio will not only allow you to attain a certain amount of calls, but this makes you aware of the committed amount of rejection needed that result in you not becoming demotivated as you get rejected. For example, your daily goal could be that you need to make thirty cold calls to get one customer meeting. Instead of feeling bad about twenty-nine rejections, the aim of achieving your ratio of twenty-nine rejections can be considered an achievement that can reduce your frustration level.

Dealing with Gatekeepers

If a CEO met with everyone who called in, they would never get their job done. Which is precisely why a gatekeeper is relevant when considering people compete for the CEO's time both inside and outside an organisation.

To reach a CEO who finally makes a decision, you will first need to get past the gatekeeper that seems to hold the key to unlock your access to the CEO. Still, you can't leave your fate in the hands of a message left with the gatekeeper.

One of the most challenging things to determine in the decision-making process is whether a particular stakeholder is a ratifier or a decision-maker. People often take up many roles in the decision-making process, and when a CEO is a ratifier, you don't need to see them, and so you might not need to speak to the gatekeeper.

If the CEO is a ratifier, they are probably going to rubber-stamp all proposals while the selection committee members are the real decision-makers. So, once you have a clear understanding of each step, including what these people decide (or influence) in each step of the decision-making process, you will have either learned that: the CEO rubber-stamp the committee's decision or the CEO looks to make the final decision themselves.

As described in chapter 14, understanding the customer's decision-making process enables salespeople to identify and speak with the right decision-makers from day one. To note though is the decision-making process in Fortune 500 and large enterprises is more a bottom-up approach whereas, in SMB and start-up organisations, it's more a top-down approach.

If the CEO makes the final decision, you'll need to speak with them, or you will be guessing about their criteria and beliefs of a solution that might never meet their needs. The reality though is you will often deal with gatekeepers, and there are no secrets that will get you past them. Still, many salespeople have identified approaches that give them an edge when dealing with gatekeepers.

Salespeople know the gatekeeper has their individual beliefs, values, concerns and motivations. Like the salesperson, they too have a boss and their job to do. They understand that gatekeepers get paid to keep salespeople from getting to decision-makers. So, the salesperson's success in getting through the gatekeeper depends on a combination of transparency, integrity, empathy, and commitment.

- **Transparency**: Tell the gatekeeper your full name and the name of your organisation. Salespeople usually let the gatekeeper know that they are calling for a meeting request with the CEO, and they have valuable insights into solving a specific business challenge. By now, you should have done your research and have a valuable reason for speaking with the CEO based on the information gathered while creating your preparation plan.
- **Integrity**: If speaking with the CEO might go against their policies, inform the gatekeeper that you can understand this situation and ask if they could think of a creative way to meet the intent of both organisations guidelines without violating them.
- **Empathy**: Showing empathy tells the gatekeeper that you acknowledge and understand their role. Tell the gatekeeper that your goal is to provide valuable insights into a solution that can solve an organisational challenge, so speaking (and meeting) with the owners of these challenges is necessary. Ask the gatekeeper what would be the best way to set up an appointment with the owners of these challenges?
- **Commitment**: Point out that each person has a unique perspective and let the gatekeeper know that you understand they don't want to waste their CEO's time. Tell the gatekeeper that instead of all the back and forth on emails, brochures and other activities that ends-up taking more time rather than less, you would only require 30min from the CEO.

Sometimes, the best way is to sidestep the gatekeeper by leveraging your social media activities. For example, sending a social media invite allows you to move right past the gatekeeper, or you may congratulate the CEO on an achievement where you have a good chance of getting a response that opens the door for further interaction. Another example of skipping past the gatekeeper is an email sent directly to the CEO with a request to meet. Today, it's easier to find an email address (or phone number) or social media account of almost anyone. You could even call the office early in the morning or late in the evening when the gatekeeper is away and where the CEO might answer incoming calls. The best and most accessible is still meeting them in person at customer events, tradeshows and other events where the CEO attends.

THE END..... *OR IS IT A NEW BEGINNING*

After a long life of observation and reflection, we usually come to the understanding that truth is subjective; my perception is thus my reality; therefore, truth is the direction of my understanding and lessons learned. Here, at the end of this book, you will carry on with your studies and professional career, or perhaps you may decide to make a life-changing decision to transform your learning curve to strategically react in both favourable and unfavourable situations as they occur. Keep in mind that understanding and application are two sides of the same coin. Therefore, the knowledge-transfer presented here can only be solidified through practice and an individual's lessons learned.

We all have different lived experiences (and world views), and we don't have to agree on everything. Yet, there is still no substitute for a willing partner who shares content that seeks to inform, inspire, and prepare individuals sufficiently for the current and projected needs. No one in this world has figured out everything, but best-practices and lessons-learned coming from an expert with a track-record can help readers form an independent opinion that may uncover new opportunities.

Like with all professions, the sales and business development are attainable roles with much gratification if you can handle the psychological aspect of dealing with the constant pressure and the inevitable peaks and valleys of being in sales. To build a legacy in your sales profession, never let someone devalue your brand and keep a positive mental attitude from now on as it costs you nothing to predict positiveness.

Where experience meets challenges, we become vigilant and better equipped to adapt to constant trying circumstances. Learning, growing, staying positive, staying connected spiritually, and getting back up on your feet are all part of human's daily struggle in life. Life is a continuous learning process and every inspirational, self-improvement book to act, achieve, and live better, including this one, should be evaluated by what happens to you, resulting from the book's power to motivate you to a desirable action. It is now your task, to see in part and predict in part on your future career trajectories that should be tailored to your inspirations and aspirations. Will you be up for the captivating and gratifying role in sales and business development?

Glossary

- **Affiliated Brands** : This term refers to organisations that are owned and controlled by a separate, third party.
- **Artificial Intelligence (AI)** : In computer science, artificial intelligence (AI), sometimes called machine intelligence, is intelligence demonstrated by machines, unlike the natural intelligence displayed by humans and animals (Wikipedia).
- **Business Model** : A business model describes the rationale of how an organisation creates, delivers, and captures value in economic, social, cultural, or other contexts (Wikipedia).
- **Business Strategy** : Business strategy can be understood as the course of action or set of decisions which assist entrepreneurs and executives to achieve specific business objectives (Business Jargons).
- **Buyer's Journey** : The buyer⊳s journey relates to the steps or choices a customer makes while researching a product to make a purchase decision. The buyer⊳s journey has three stages, awareness, consideration, and selection.
- **Cobots** : Cobots (or collaborative robots) are robots intended for direct human robot interaction within a shared space, or where humans and robots are in close proximity (Wikipedia).
- **Collaborative Intelligence** : Collaborative intelligence is a term used in several disciplines. In business it describes heterogeneous networks of people interacting to produce intelligent outcomes. It characterises multi-agent, distributed systems where each agent, human, or machine is uniquely positioned with autonomy to contribute to a problem-solving network.
- **Collaborative Leadership** : Collaborative leadership is a management practice that aims to bring managers, executives and staff out of silos to work together. In collaborative workplaces, information is shared organically and everyone takes responsibility for the whole (slackhq.com).
- **Corporate Culture** : Corporate culture refers to the beliefs and behaviours that determine how a company's employees and management interact and handle outside business transactions (Investopedia).
- **CRM** : Customer relationship management is an approach to managing a

company's interactions with current and potential customers (Wikipedia).

- **Cutting-Edge Technology** : Cutting-edge technology refers to technological devices, techniques or achievements that employ the most current and high-level IT developments; in other words, technology at the frontiers of knowledge. Leading and innovative IT industry organizations are often referred to as «cutting edge.» (Techopedia).
- **ERP** : Enterprise resource planning is the integrated management of main business processes, often in real time and mediated by software and technology (Wikipedia).
- **Fourth Industrial Revolution (or Industry 4.0)** : Industry 4.0 is the ongoing automation of traditional manufacturing and industrial practices, using modern smart technology. Large-scale machine-to-machine communication (M2M) and the internet of things (IoT) are integrated for increased automation, improved communication and self-monitoring, and production of smart machines that can analyse and diagnose issues without the need for human intervention (Wikipedia).
- **Information and communications technology (ICT)** : Information and communications technology (ICT) are an extensional term for information technology (IT) that stresses the role of unified communications and the integration of telecommunications (telephone lines and wireless signals) and computers, as well as necessary enterprise software, middleware, storage, and audio-visual systems, that enable users to access, store, transmit, and manipulate information (Wikipedia).
- **Holacracy** : Holacracy is a method of decentralized management and organizational governance, in which authority and decision-making are distributed throughout a holarchy of self-organizing teams rather than being vested in a management hierarchy (Wikipedia).
- **KPI** : Key performance indicator (KPI) is a type of performance measurement. KPIs evaluate the success of an organisation or of a particular activity (such as projects, programs, products and other initiatives) in which it engages (Wikipedia).
- **LE** : A large enterprise meets at least one of the following conditions: it has at least 5000 employees; or it has an annual turnover greater than 1.5 billion euros and a balance sheet total of more than 2 billion euros (Insee).
- **M&A** : Mergers & acquisitions are transactions in which the ownership of companies, other business organisations, or their operating units is transferred or consolidated with other entities (Huxley).
- **Net Promoter Score (NPS)** : Net Promoter Score is a management tool that

can be used to gauge the loyalty of a firm›s customer relationships. It serves as an alternative to traditional customer satisfaction research and is claimed to be correlated with revenue growth (Wikipedia).

- **Neuromarketing** : Neuromarketing is a commercial marketing communication field that applies neuropsychology to marketing research, studying consumers› sensorimotor, cognitive, and affective response to marketing stimuli. Neuromarketing seeks to understand the rationale behind how consumers make purchasing decisions and their responses to marketing stimuli in order to apply those learnings in the marketing realm (Wikipedia).
- **Operational Excellence** : Operational excellence is the execution of an organisation's business strategy more consistently and reliably than the competition. It is determined by the results (BTOES).
- **Organisation** : An organisation is an entity comprising multiple people, such as an institution, company, or association, that has a particular purpose (Wikipedia).
- **PE firms** : A private equity firm is an investment management company that provides financial backing and makes investments in the private equity of start-ups or operating companies through a variety of loosely affiliated investment strategies including leveraged buyout, venture capital, and growth capital (Wikipedia).
- **PO** : A purchase order is the first official offer issued by a buyer to a seller indicating types, quantities, and agreed-upon prices for products or services (Wikipedia).
- **Procrastination**: Procrastination is the action of delaying or postponing something. Although typically perceived as a negative trait due to its hindering effect on one's productivity often associated with depression, low self-esteem, guilt and inadequacy, it can also be considered a wise response to certain demands that could present risky or negative outcomes or require waiting for new information to arrive (Wikipedia).
- **Purchase decision-making process** : The consumer purchase decision-making process is divided into five stages. These include problem recognition, information search, evaluation of alternatives, purchase decision, and post-purchase evaluation (scitechnol).
- **Sales Pipeline** : Sales pipelines are forecasts of potential business opportunities that salespeople have identified to reach their sales quota. A sales pipeline illustrates where prospects or business opportunities are in the sales cycle. Their win probability is noted as a percentage, along with expected dates to close these deals.
- **Sales Strategy** : A sales strategy is a plan a business or individual makes to sell

products and services and increase profits (Chron).

- **SME** : Small and medium-sized enterprises (SMEs) employ fewer than 250 persons and have an annual turnover not exceeding 50 million euro, and/or an annual balance sheet total not exceeding 43 million euro (Eurostat).
- **Solution Selling (or Conceptual Sales)** : Solution selling is a type and style of sales and selling methodology. Solution selling has a salesperson or sales team use a sales process that is a problem-led approach to determine if and how a change in a product could bring specific improvements that are desired by the customer (Wikipedia). Conceptual selling refers to raising awareness of the

  benefits or USPs and is founded on the principles that customers don't buy a product or a service, they buy an end-to-end concept of a solution offering.
- **SOW** : Share of wallet is a survey method used in performance management to measure how much of a company's spending on a certain product category goes to a particular business-to-business (B2B) vendor (Iammoulude).
- **Technical Representative (TR)** : A technical representative gives advice on the application, installation, operation, and maintenance of an organisation's products, in addition to selling the products. In most organisations, salespeople manage the value proposition and negotiations to close the deal, while the technical representatives put the value proposition into physical practice.
- **Time To Market (TTM)** : In commerce, time to market is the length of time it takes from a product being conceived until it's being available for sale. TTM is important in industries where products are outmoded quickly (Wikipedia).
- **Transformative Innovation** : Transformative innovation is a core concept in creating business models that are profitable, competitive and long-lasting. In effect, transformational innovation is changes that shift the entire system into a new framework, that is created to be viable for the future (Highalphainno).
- **Value Proposition** : A promise of the value to be delivered. This term can apply to entire companies or individual products, and in the latter case, it is used by salespeople to close deals with their customers.
- **Visual Communication** : Visual communication conveys ideas and information in forms that can be seen, static and digital. These include signs, typography, drawing, graphic design, illustration, industrial design, advertising, animation, colour, and electronic resources (Wikipedia).

Bibliography

Aldo Canizales with Mr. Choice. (2019) To Fetch a Lead: Guide to Lead Generation for B2B Companies.

Amazon. Leadership Principles.

Ambition. The Winner's Guide to Effective Sales Coaching.

Anxiety Disorders Association of America (ADAA). (2006) Stress & Anxiety Disorders Survey. Highlights: Workplace Stress & Anxiety Disorders Survey.

Art Sobczak. (2010) Smart Calling: Eliminate the Fear, Failure, and Rejection from Cold Calling.

Axonify. (2018) Axonify Finds No Improvement in Corporate Training in Second Annual State of Workplace Training Study: According to Study, an Alarming One-Third of U.S. Adult Employees Don't Receive Formal Job Training.

Business Events Council of Australia (BECA). (2020) Value of Business Events to Australia.

Cape Peninsula University of Technology. (2018) Multiple Stakeholders' Perceptions of the Impacts of a Carnival in Cape Town.

Carl Gustav Jung. (1921) Psychological Types - Translation by H. Godwyn Baynes (1923).

Carol S Fleming P.h.D. (2013) It's the Way You Say It - Second Edition: Becoming Articulate, Well-Spoken, and Clear.

Catherine Clifford. (2015) Unhappy Workers Cost the U.S. Up to $550 Billion a Year (Infographic).

Centers for Disease Control and Prevention. (2016) Workplace Health Promotion: Depression Evaluation Measures.

Charlotte Lieberman. (2019) Why You Procrastinate (It Has Nothing to Do With Self-Control): If procrastination isn't about laziness, then what is it about?

Chris Myers. (2017) Three Reasons Why Sales People Make The Best CEOs.

City of Munich - Department of Labor and Economic Develoment. (2019) A business perspective: The economic impact of the Oktoberfest.

Daniel R. Denison. (2018) Bringing Corporate Culture to the Bottom Line.

David Egan. (2018) Here Is What It Takes to Become a CEO, According to 12,000 LinkedIn Profiles.

Deloitte. (2020) The Deloitte Global Millennial Survey: Millennials and Gen Zs hold the key to creating a "better normal".

Denise Lee Yohn. (2018) Engaging Employees Starts with Remembering What Your Company Stands For.

Derek Hutson. (2018) So, You're in Sales But (Secretly) Yearn to be a CEO. Here's How to Make That Happen. For starters, you're in good company: Warren Buffett, Mark Cuban and Howard Schultz all started in sales.

Dr. Pychyl and Dr. Sirois. (2013) This is a repository copy of Procrastination and the Priority of Short-Term Mood Regulation: Consequences for Future Self.

Entrepreneur. (2008) Howard Schultz: Starbucks' First Mate.

Fred E. Miller. (2011) No Sweat Public Speaking!": How to Develop, Practice and Deliver a Knock Your Socks Off! Presentation with - No Sweat!

Frederick E. Allen. (2012) The Zen at the Heart of Steve Jobs' Genius.

G. Dautovic. (2020) Big Game, Big Spending: 25 Super Bowl Revenue Statistics.

Gallup. (2013) State of the American Workplace: Employee Engagement Insights for U.S. Business Leaders.

Glassdoor. (2017) Statistical Reference Guide for Reruiters: 50 HR and Recruiting Statistics for 2017.

Glenn Llopis. (2014) 5 Ways A Legacy-Driven Mindset Will Define Your Leadership.

Imperative and LinkedIn: (2016) Workforce Purpose Index. Purpose at Work: The Largest Global Study on the Role of Purpose in the Workforce.

James Brady. (2017) Floyd Mayweather's 50 wins, ranked: Floyd Mayweather is 50-0 after beating Conor McGregor, and we ranked every single fight of his illustrious career.

Janet E. Esposito. (2005) In The SpotLight: Overcome Your Fear of Public Speaking and Performing.

Jeff Murphy. (2017) The 2017 State of Workplace Culture Report.

Jeff Thull. (2010) Mastering the Complex Sale (second edition): How to Compete and Win when the Stakes are High!

Jesper B. Sørensen - Massachusetts Institute of Technology. (2001) The Strength of Corporate Culture and the Reliability of Firm Performance. Running Head: "Culture and Reliability.

John Wade. (2008) Persuasion in Negotiation and Mediation.

Joseph Messinger. (2004) Ces gestes qui vous trahissent.

Joseph Murphy. (2009) The Power of Your Subconscious Mind.

Julie Koprowska.(2010) Communication and Interpersonal Skills in Social Work (Transforming Social Work Practice Series).

Ken Favaro, Per-Ola Karlsson, and Gary L. Neilson. (2014) The Lives and Times of the CEO. From 100 years back to a quarter century ahead, the evolution of the chief executive officer.

Kenneth L. Higher P.h.D. (2001) Your Memory: How It Works and How to Improve It.

Kotaro Hara, Abi Adams, Kristy Milland, Saiph Savage, Chris Callison-Burch, Jeffrey P. Bigham. (2018) Data-Driven Analysis of Workers' Earnings on Amazon

Mechanical Turk.

Leah Ginsberg. (2017) How Mark Cuban started with just $60 in his pocket and became a billionaire.

Lee Chyen Yee and Clare Jim publication with Thomson Reuters. (2011) Foxconn to rely more on robots; could use 1 million in 3 years.

Lovely Professional University. (2013) Essentials of Organisation Behaviour.

Malcolm Higgs and Deborah Rowland. (2000) Building change leadership capability: 'The quest for change competence'.

Manish Kumar, Himanshu Rai, and Surya Prakash Pati. (2009) An Exploratory Study on Negotiating Styles: Development of a Measure.

McKinsey Global Institute (MGI). (2017) Jobs lost, Jobs gained: Workforce Transitions in a time of Automation.

Michal Bohanes. (2018) 'Following Your Passion' Is Dead - Here's What To Replace It With.

Neil Thomson. (2011) Effective Communication: A Guide for the People Professions.

Nick Hedges. (2015) From Sales Rep to CEO: 5 Reasons Salespeople Make Great LeadersHow a sales background can lay the foundation for a strong leader.

Officevibe. (2016) The Global & Real-Time State Of Employee Engagement.

People At Their Best. Business Development - Perspectives for Uncovering & Closing New Business Opportunities

PricewaterhouseCoopers (PWC). (2018) Will robots really steal our jobs? An international analysis of the potential long term impact of automation.

R. Pawan Kumar. 8 CEOs who were once sales reps.

Richard Fry. (2018) Millennials are the largest generation in the U.S. labor force. Pew Research Center.

Richard Rumney. (2011) Good Strategy/Bad Strategy: The Difference and Why It Matters.

Rick Skarin. From Tech Salesperson to Tech CEO: Technology firm bosses with sales backgrounds are a rarity. A new Korn Ferry report suggests why that should change.

Rob Steffens. (2018) How to Build an Infectious Company Culture.

Robert B. Caldini. (2006) Influence: The Psychology of Persuasion.

Sam Richter. (2008) Take the Cold Out of Cold Calling.

Spiro. (2017) 7 Reasons why being a Salesperson will make you a better CEO.

Statista. (2019) Revenue of the tourism and services sector during Carnival in Brazil from 2012 to 2020.

Stephan Shiffman. (2007) Cold Calling Techniques: That Really Work.

Susan Sorenson with Gallup. (2013) How Employee Engagement Drives Growth.

The Execu|Search Group. (2018) Talent Engagement Will be Critical To Combating the Skills Shortage in 2018, According to New Hiring Outlook Report by The

Execu|Search Group.

Thomson Reuters. (2019) China Lunar New Year retail sales rise, but pace slowest in years.

Tony Alessandra, Scott Michael Zimmerman and Joseph La Lopa. (2009) The Platinum Rule for Sales Mastery Paperback.

Udemy In Depth. (2018) Coping with Workplace Distractions: A Learning Culture Can Help People Work Smarter.

Upland » Altify. (2016) Altify Knowledge Study Finds 74 Percent of Sellers Increase Win Rates with Account Planning.

Victor Daniels. (2011) The Analytical Psychology of Carl Gustav Jung.

"Waverly Deutsch. (2018). What great entrepreneurs, salespeople, and business leaders have in common: There are some key similarities . . . and differences.

William R. Steele. (2009) Presentation Skills 201: How to Take It to the Next Level as a Confident, Engaging Presenter.

Work Institute. (2018) Retention Report: Truth & Trends in Turnover.

Zack Guzman and Mary Stevens. (2017) Here's how Warren Buffett hustled to make $53,000 as a teenager.

www.ingramcontent.com/pod-product-compliance
Ingram Content Group UK Ltd.
Pitfield, Milton Keynes, MK11 3LW, UK
UKHW021914190726
13853UKWH00002B/667

9 783952 517482